BUREAU OF INTERNATIONAL RESEARCH
HARVARD UNIVERSITY AND
RADCLIFFE COLLEGE
HARVARD STUDIES IN INTERNATIONAL LAW

MANLEY O. HUDSON, *Editor*

No. 1. The International Protection of Trade Marks by the American Republics

By Stephen P. Ladas, D.N., A.M., LL.B., S.J.D.

LONDON: HUMPHREY MILFORD
OXFORD UNIVERSITY PRESS

THE INTERNATIONAL PROTECTION OF TRADE MARKS BY THE AMERICAN REPUBLICS

BY

STEPHEN P. LADAS

BUREAU OF INTERNATIONAL RESEARCH
OF HARVARD UNIVERSITY AND RADCLIFFE COLLEGE

CAMBRIDGE
HARVARD UNIVERSITY PRESS
1929

The Bureau of International Research has aided the author in carrying on research and in publishing the results. The Bureau assumes no responsibility for any statements or views expressed.

THE MURRAY PRINTING COMPANY
CAMBRIDGE, MASSACHUSETTS

Printed in United States of America

PREFACE

This study of the problems of Inter-American trade mark protection and repression of unfair competition is published primarily with the hope that it may facilitate the work of the conference of trade mark experts and specialists of the American countries, meeting at Washington, February 11, 1929. The author has prepared a study of international protection of industrial property in general, which will soon be published under the auspices of the Bureau of International Research of Harvard University and Radcliffe College. The forthcoming conference in Washington seems to justify the publication of this more limited study. The author has had the benefit of conferences with eminent trade mark experts, in particular with Mr. Lawrence Langner of New York City, to whom he wishes to acknowledge his indebtedness.

S. P. Ladas.

Cambridge, Massachusetts,
February 1, 1929.

CONTENTS

THE INTERNATIONAL PROTECTION OF TRADE MARKS BY THE AMERICAN REPUBLICS

THE INTERNATIONAL PROTECTION OF TRADE MARKS BY THE AMERICAN REPUBLICS

I

THE INTERNATIONAL PROTECTION OF INDUSTRIAL PROPERTY

INDUSTRIAL property is a collective name for various interests springing out of the commercial and industrial activity of man that are considered today equally important and valuable as those in tangible objects. These various interests may be divided into two classes: (*a*) legal monopolies and (*b*) advantageous business relations.

Patents of invention, working models and industrial designs and models are legal monopolies. The law recognizes to their authors the privilege of exclusive use or exploitation of their respective creations for a limited period. This is due to a policy of encouraging improvements of industry by which the community profits. At the lapse of this period the public becomes possessed of the invention, design or model.

Trade marks, trade names, statements as to place of origin and other distinctive signs used in connection with the commercial or industrial organization of a manufacturer, merchant or agriculturist are vehicles of advantageous business relations. They are devices used by the latter to protect, maintain and extend their activities and their association with the public. They are not creations in the same sense as inventions or designs and models.

The genesis and development of the various industrial

property rights, generally speaking, does not date back further than the 19th century. It coincides with the development of machinery, commerce and communication. The law had to be put into harmony with life. The same policy of encouraging the progress and at the same time avoiding an excessive restriction on the freedom of commerce and industry was imposed on the legislator in each country.

However, the same conditions of industrial and commercial life were not found everywhere. The pressure of interests was not alike in all countries. Their dissimilar recognition and delimitation produced a differentiation of law. Besides, the traditional technique in handling legal materials and analogous legal principles, and the administrative practice are largely responsible for divergences between the law of industrial property in the various countries.

Yet, many countries felt the need of making use of experience and knowledge acquired in other countries possessing before them legislation on industrial property rights. They were led to adopt the general principles and the regulation of those countries, whose general law and legal phraseology were akin to their own. Thus, there has resulted a distinction of the law of the various countries in regard to its underlying ideas as well as to its general principles and the administrative regulation into three general groups, constituted by the English speaking countries, the Latin countries (France, Italy, Spain, Latin America, etc.) and the Germanic or Northern European countries (Germany, Austria, the Netherlands, Norway, Sweden, etc.).

The legislative activity in this respect in the various countries is far from being a complete edifice of law of industrial property. It has been based on practical utility and determined by the needs of each time. A general view of the interests, claims and demands to be satisfied and a systematic process of seeking to adjust, harmonize and secure them has often been lacking. It is only in recent years that the whole matter of industrial property has formed the subject of systematic juristic[1] and legislative[2] ordering.

The divergences and defects of municipal law of the various countries affected especially foreigners. They were either deprived definitely of some rights which nationals

[1] See especially: Allfeld, *Grundriss des Gewerblichen Rechtsschutzes*, Leipzig, 1910, and *Urheber- und Erfinderrecht*, Berlin, 1923; Breuer Moreno, *Derecho Intelectual Comparado*, Buenos Aires, 1921; Bry, *La Propriété Industrielle, Littéraire et Artistique*, 3rd ed., Paris, 1914; Cairo, *Moderni Regolamenti Giuridici della Proprietà Industriale*, Milano, 1926; Elster, *Gewerblicher Rechtsschutz*, Berlin, 1921; Huard, *Traité de la Propriété Intellectuelle*, 2 vols., Paris, 1903–1906; Kohler's books on various rights of industrial property and his *Studien zur Förderung des Gewerblichen Rechtsschutzes*, Berlin, 1908; Osterrieth, *Lehrbuch des Gewerblichen Rechtsschutzes*, Leipzig, 1908; Pillet, *Le Régime International de la Propriété Industrielle*, Paris, 1911.

[2] Portugal, Law of May 21, 1896, on Industrial Property (*Collecção Oficial* 1896, p. 402).

Costa Rica, Decree No. 40 of June 27, 1896 on Intellectual Property (*Colleccion de Leyes y Decretos 1896*, p. 201).

Spain, Law of May 16, 1902, on Industrial Property (*Legislación*, 1902, II, p. 88).

Morocco, Act of June 23, 1916, on Industrial Property (*Propriété Industrielle*, 1917, pp. 3, 18, 37, 60).

Serb-Croat-Slovene State, Royal Decree of November 15, 1920 and Law of February 17, 1922 on Industrial Property. (*Propriété Industrielle*, 1921, p. 34 and 1922, p. 61).

Brazil, Decree No. 16264 of December 19, 1923 for the creation of a General Direction of Industrial Property and Annexed *Regulamento* under same date (*Collecção das Leis da Republica des Estados Unidos do Brazil de 1923*, vol. III, p. 330).

Syria and Lebanon, Decree No. 2385 of January 17, 1924, organizing the protection of Commercial, Industrial, Literary and Artistic Property (*Bulletin Officiel du Haut Commissariat, 3e année*, February, 1924).

Poland, Law of February 5, 1924, on Patents, Designs and Trade Marks and Law of August 2, 1926 on Unfair Competition (*Propriété Industrielle*, 1924, pp. 198, 221, 245, and 1927, p. 8).

Colombia, Law No. 31 of February 28, 1925 on Industrial Property (*República de Colombia, Leyes* 1925, p. 81).

Irish Free State Industrial and Commercial property (Protection) Act, 1927 (*Saorstát Eireann*, Number 16 of 1927).

A recasting of the separate laws on patents, designs, trade marks, etc. into an organic law embracing all industrial property rights is under preparation in Italy (see *Propriété Industrielle*, 1926, pp. 154, 173).

enjoyed, or were subject to special obligations. In other cases the protection of their rights was conditional upon the existence of reciprocity. And even when foreigners were entitled by the law to the same protection as nationals, such protection could not be enjoyed in fact. They suffered from the diversities and opposition of law itself. For instance, their application for a patent in one country, giving publicity to the invention, destroyed its novelty for the other countries where no valid patent could be granted in such case. Also a trade mark lawful and registrable, according to the law of one country, could not be protected and registered in the same form in another.

The attempts, from the middle of the last century, to secure international protection through provisions to this effect, inserted in treaties of commerce or special bipartite agreements, did not prove satisfactory. The previous disparity and uncertainty was in no way diminished since the municipal law was hardly derogated from by these agreements. Besides, the latter followed the instability inherent in commercial treaties.

The Union for the Protection of Industrial Property

The rational international regulation and protection of industrial property as well as the great development of the law and theory of industrial property was brought about by the creation of the *Union for the Protection of Industrial Property* constituted in 1883 by the International Convention signed at Paris on March 20. The member countries of this Union which originally numbered eleven are now thirty-eight and include the American countries: Brazil, Cuba, the Dominican Republic, Mexico, and the United States. Great Britain which is also a member of the Union has acceded to the convention in behalf, among others, of Canada and Trinidad and Tobago. An Arrangement for the international registration of trade marks was signed at Madrid in 1891 by some of the members of the Union and includes today twenty-two countries, among them: Brazil, Cuba, and Mexico. The first two are also members of another restricted Union constituted by the Arrangement for the repression of false indications of origin, signed also at Madrid in 1891 and now including fourteen countries. At the last Conference of The Hague, in 1925, a new Arrangement for the international deposit of industrial designs and models was signed by representatives of ten countries.[1]

The Industrial Property Union, as its title indicates, is concerned with the protection of all industrial property rights, i.e., patents, working models, industrial designs and models, trade marks, trade names, statements of place of origin, and with the protection against acts of unfair competition. To this end it contains three kinds of stipulations: an important number of provisions constitute common legislation for all member countries and need no municipal law to carry them into effect; others are only stipulations of principle or engagements of the members and need legislative action by each country; and others refer to the municipal law of each country which they do not seek to influence in any way.

The fundamental principle of the Union is that of national treatment; namely, in each of the member countries the nationals of the others, as also all persons domiciled or possessing industrial or commercial establishments in the Union, enjoy the same advantages, rights, remedies, and protection that are now granted or will be granted in the future to nationals of that country. In addition to this, however, the same persons enjoy the specific rights provided for by the convention. Namely, for patents: (1) a right of priority of

[1] See text of these acts as revised at The Hague in 41 *La Propriété Industrielle* (1925) 221. The first two form appendices III and IV of this study.

one year from the date of filing of a patent application in a country of the Union for the purpose of filing in the other countries; (2) independence of the patent rights granted to the same person for the same invention in several member countries; (3) prohibition of forfeiture of the patent by reason of importation of patented articles in the country where the patent was granted; (4) restriction of the obligation to work the patent in each country where one was granted; (5) a period of grace of six months for the payment of fees and taxes or one of three months and a right of restoration of the forfeited patent.

The specific rights granted by the convention for industrial designs and models are similar to the rights under numbers (1) and (3) enumerated above with respect to patents, and a three month period of grace. By the countries parties to the Arrangement of The Hague the additional privilege of international deposit of designs and models is enjoyed. Trade names enjoy the benefit of a provision of the convention to the effect that no deposit or registration is necessary for their protection and that they are protected whether or not they form part of a trade mark. Moreover certain specific effective remedies of repression are provided for against their infringement.

For the protection of trade marks the following specific rights are granted by the convention: (1) a right of priority of six months for registration in other countries after filing an application for registration of a trade mark in the country of origin; (2) restriction of the obligation to use the mark within each country; (3) a three month period of grace for payment of fees and taxes; (4) validation of trade marks in their original form in the member countries after their registration in the country of origin, subject to certain well-defined exceptions; (5) a right to request the rejection or cancellation of a mark well-known to belong to a *ressortis-*

sant of another member country; (6) specific effective remedies of repression against infringement of trade marks.

The same effective remedies of repression are provided for against false indications of origin and acts of unfair competition. The Madrid arrangement for the repression of false indications of origin purports to afford a larger protection in this respect. A definition of unfair competition is included in the convention and certain acts are enumerated against which the member countries are bound to afford protection.

The Madrid arrangement for the international registration of trade marks enables persons entitled to its benefits to register their marks at the International Bureau of the Union after registration in the country of origin. The Bureau gives notice of such registration to the member countries, which may refuse protection only within a year from such notice and only for the reasons provided for in the exceptions to the principle of validation of marks contained in the general convention. By such registration, trade mark owners enjoy the same protection they would enjoy by a direct registration in each of the contracting countries. But the duration of the protection in each of them is uniform: twenty years from the date of international registration. No other fees are payable, except 100 Swiss francs for the international registration.[1]

The Union is made a living organism through its International Bureau established at Berne. One cannot praise too much the work and the accomplishments of this Bureau. But this is not the place to describe them. Sufficient to say that the application and execution of the convention is made more effective through its activities, and that through its collections of the laws, administrative practices and judicial decisions of the member countries, and its special studies

[1] This fee was raised to 150 francs at the conference at The Hague in 1925. But the fee for each additional mark is seventy-five francs. Either may be paid in two instalments.

on numerous questions of industrial property in its monthly periodical *La Propriété Industrielle*, now entering its 44th year, it has been of incalculable aid to interested parties, has promoted a conscientious preparation of the revisions of the convention and arrangements, and is helping the progressive uniformity of the law.

II

HISTORY OF PAN AMERICAN CONVENTIONS ON INDUSTRIAL PROPERTY

THE International Convention for the protection of industrial property exercised its influence on the municipal law of the various countries and on the conventional regime of countries which did not belong to the Union. An outstanding illustration in the latter respect is afforded by the efforts of American States to achieve an Inter-American protection of industrial property. These efforts began forty years ago.

1. Early Conventions

In 1889 at the International Congress of South American States at Montevideo, in connection with the other efforts at achieving uniformity in the law governing the international relations of these states, two conventions were signed on January 16, concerning patents and trade marks.[1] The contracting countries in these conventions are Argentina, Bolivia, Chile, Paraguay, Peru, and Uruguay. All ratified them with the exception of Bolivia and Chile. These conventions secured reciprocal national treatment to the patentees and trade mark owners of the contracting countries and a right of priority of one year for patents only. In all other respects they referred to the municipal law of each country. The outstanding feature of these conventions is that they contained a definition of patentable inventions and trade marks.

The first Pan American Conference, which was held a few months later in Washington, recommended to the other

[1] See text of the Conventions in 2 *Tratados, Convenciones, Protocolos de la República Argentina* (1901), pp. 120 and 127. See also XVIII *De Martens, N. R., 2me Sér.* 421 and 453.

American countries the adoption of the Montevideo Conventions.[1]

At the Second International Conference of American States, at Mexico City, a new convention was signed on January 27, 1902, on patents, industrial drawings and models and trade marks.[2] This convention adopted most of the provisions of the two Montevideo Conventions and borrowed certain provisions from the International Convention of 1883. It also authorized the consular agents of the country to which owners of patents, designs or trade marks belonged, to act as legal representatives for such owners in complying with the formalities and conditions required at the filing of applications.

This convention was ratified only by the five Central American countries: Guatemala, Salvador, Costa Rica, Honduras, and Nicaragua, and by Cuba.[3] But as between the former it was abrogated by Article XX of the Treaty of Peace of Washington on December 20, 1907,[4] which put an end to the war between Central American countries.[5]

At the Third Conference of American States, meeting at Rio de Janeiro in July, 1906, the drafting of a new Pan American Convention was decided upon, against the opinion of the Mexican delegation that all American States should accede to the Industrial Property Union constituted by the International convention of 1883.[6] A new convention,

[1] Sen. Doc. 177, 51st Cong., 1st Sess.

[2] See text of convention in Spanish, English and French in *Second Pan American Conference, Minutes and Documents*, Mexico, 1902, pp. 723 ff.

[3] See VI *De Martens, N. R., 3me Sér.* 206; also *Fifth International Conference of American States, Handbook of the Pan American Union*, Washington, 1922, p. 10.

[4] Ratified by all the signatory states, February and March, 1908. See 100 *Br. & For. St. Papers*, 835.

[5] See "*La Protection internationale de la propriété intellectuelle dans l'Amérique Centrale*" in 27 *Propriété Industrielle*, 1911, p. 50.

[6] See *Tercera Conferencia Internacional Americana, Actas, Resoluciones, Documentos*, Rio de Janeiro, 1907, pp. 105, 249, 275, 641.

adopted and signed on August 9, concerned conjointly patents of invention, drawings and industrial models, trade marks and literary and artistic property. It incorporated the conventions of 1902 and added a number of important amendments thereto, the purpose of which was to create a Union between the American States for the protection of intellectual property. To this end two Inter-American Bureaus were to be created, one at Havana and the other at Rio de Janeiro.

In the establishment of these bureaus the convention of 1906 followed the Madrid arrangement of 1891 for the international registration of trade marks; yet, it went much further in purporting to centralize the registrations of literary and artistic works, patents, and designs and models, as well as of trade marks. No uniform duration of protection was provided for, and the fee for the international registration was to be five dollars. However, it has not been possible to organize the Inter-American Bureaus provided for by this convention, as the latter was not ratified by two thirds at least of the contracting countries, as it was stipulated.[1] Indeed, it was clear that the provisions of the convention concerning the international registration at the Inter-American Bureaus could not be executed. The question of international filing of patents or patent applications presented too serious difficulties and too many complications to be accomplished by the indefinite and vague provisions of this convention. The Brazilian review, *Patentes y Marcas*, warned the governments of the American countries as soon as the convention was signed that "the convention will not come into effect because it is not practical and useful for commerce and industry; to centralize the services at Habana

[1] The convention was ratified by eight countries: Chile, Costa Rica, Ecuador, Guatemala, Honduras, Panama, Nicaragua, and Salvador. See VI *De Martens, N. R., 3me Sér.*, 221, and *Fourth International Conference of American States*, Sen. Doc. 744, 61st Cong., 3d Sess., p. 98.

and at Rio de Janeiro is not at all to centralize them; and to limit the unification to America in this dualistic form is a task which is not worth prosecuting when it is much simpler to accede to the Industrial Property Union of 1883."[1]

2. The Conventions of 1910

When the Fourth International Conference of American States met at Buenos Aires in July, 1910, and new conventions on patents and trade marks were proposed, the Argentine delegate, Dr. Zeballos, reluctantly concurred in the idea of Inter-American Conventions on these matters, preferring instead that the American countries should accede to the International Convention of 1883, thus avoiding the difficulties introduced by the formation of different unions and promoting the tendency towards the universal unity of definitions and juridical conceptions on a subject transcending national boundaries. On his recommendation, the committee urged that the Conventions should adopt the bases of the Industrial Property Union so as to achieve the universal uniformity of principles.[2] Under these conditions, two conventions, one relating to patents and industrial designs and models and the other concerning the protection of trade marks, were adopted by the conference without much discussion.[3] Both conventions were signed by all the states of the Pan American Union, with the exception of Bolivia, on August 20, 1910. They were ratified by Brazil, Costa Rica, Cuba, the Dominican Republic, Ecuador, Guatemala, Haiti, Honduras, Nicaragua, Panama, Paraguay, the United States, and Uruguay. The Trade Marks Con-

[1] Quoted by the *Propriété Industrielle*, 1907, pp. 129, 130.

[2] *Cuarta Conferencia Internacional Americana*, Buenos Aires, 1911, Vol. I, pp. 340–343 and 396.

[3] See texts in Spanish, English, Portuguese and French in 38 Stat. at L. Pt. 2, p. 1811, and 39 Stat. at L. Pt. 2, p. 1675; also in Spanish only in *Cuarta Conferencia Internacional Americana*, Vol. I, pp. 493 and 507.

vention was ratified also by Peru.[1] But the Governments of Costa Rica, Guatemala, Honduras, and Nicaragua subsequently denounced the Convention concerning Trade Marks after giving the notice of one year required by the terms of Article 19.[2]

The convention relating to patents and industrial designs and models ties together provisions, not always consistent,[3] of the International Convention of 1883 and of the previous Pan American Conventions. The international registration of patents, provided for by the previous convention, is discarded. Instead, the principles of national treatment, right of priority, and independence of patents of the Industrial Property Union are adopted.

The persons who may claim protection under the convention are not only nationals or *ressortissants* of the contracting countries, but "any person" who shall obtain a patent in one of the signatory states. Articles 6 and 7 undertake to define what is a patentable invention and when may a patent be refused recognition. These provisions, however, do not bind the contracting countries and are otherwise of little value. But they consider industrial designs as

[1] Both conventions were ratified by: Brazil, November 9, 1914; Costa Rica, August 7, 1915; Dominican Republic, April 18, 1912; Ecuador, November 4, 1913; Guatemala, April 27, 1912; Honduras, February 13, 1913; Nicaragua, April 23, 1912; Panama, June 12, 1913; Paraguay, August 22, 1913; United States, March 21, 1911; Uruguay, August 7, 1919.

Cuba ratified the Patent Convention on December 23, 1912, and the Trade Mark Convention on June 2, 1914.

Haiti ratified the Patent Convention on October 8, 1918, and the Trade Mark Convention on October 31, 1918.

Peru ratified the Trade Mark Convention on April 19, 1920.

[2] See *Fifth International Conference of American States, Handbook of the Pan American Union*, Washington, 1922, p. 16. Guatemala notified its withdrawal March 18, 1920; Nicaragua, July 16, 1920; Costa Rica, September 30, 1921; Honduras, February 17, 1922.

[3] For instance, Article 3, concerning the period of priority, and Article 5, concerning the moment from which priority begins. Also Articles 8 and 9 taken from the Convention of Montevideo speak only of patents, whereas the convention of 1910 concerns also industrial designs or models.

inventions in consonance with the definition given in the United States Revised Statutes, Sec. 4929, and in opposition to the general view that they constitute aesthetic creations calling for the application of totally different rules and criteria from those admitted in the case of patentable inventions.[1]

The convention concerning the protection of trade marks attempts to institute the principle of the so-called automatic registration. Every mark registered in any of the contracting countries shall be considered as also registered in the others, with the qualification, however, "without prejudice to the rights of third persons and to the provisions of the law of each state governing the same." This broad reservation practically nullifies the principle of automatic registration, since the provisions of the law of each country are not derogated from in any way. Moreover, the benefit of this provision may only be enjoyed if the registrant pays, in addition to the fees or charges fixed by the laws of the state in which application for registration is first made, the sum of fifty dollars gold for the expenses of the respective Inter-American Bureau. The English text reads: "which sum shall cover all the expenses of both Bureaus for the international registration in all the signatory States," but a correct translation of the Spanish, Portuguese and French texts would read as follows: "which sum is destined to cover the expenses of the International Registry of the respective Bureau."[2] Whatever the text be, the implication is that the marks registered in any of the contracting countries should be communicated to the respective Inter-American Bureau.

[1] See Allen, *Design Patentability*, 9 *Journal of Patent Office Society* (1927), 298; cf. 7 (1926), *ibid.*, 540; Coppieters, *Protection des Œuvres d'art appliqué*, Bruxelles, 1919, pp. 10, 32; and 25 *La Propriété Industrielle* (1919), 155, 172.

[2] The originals are as follows: "*que se destinará á cubrir los gastos de Registro Internacional de la respectiva Oficina*"; "*que se destinará para cobrir as despezas do registro internacional da respectiva Secretaria*"; "*qui sera destinée à couvrir les dépenses du Registre International du Bureau respectif.*"

But the convention in this respect is entirely indefinite and vague. The question of transmission of copies of registered marks to the Bureau, their communication to the contracting countries, and the whole scheme of protection through such communcation are hardly indicated.

What also makes the assumption of automatic registration prove ineffective is the proviso to Article 5 which leaves ultimately to the determination of the law of each state the question of the subject-matter of a trade mark. Thus a trade mark owner registering his mark in one country and resting with the assurance of its being protected automatically in the other countries may later be denied protection of his mark on the ground that it is not in consonance with domestic legislation. The advantage of a single registration is offset by the danger of the free infringement of the mark in other countries.

The protection of the convention may be claimed by "any person" who has registered his mark in any of the contracting countries. Thus a British manufacturer may register his mark in the United States and claim the benefit of the convention in all the other American countries.[1]

Persons not content with the automatic protection through the single registration and payment of the fifty dollar fee for the communication to the Inter-American Bureaus, may register their marks directly in each of the contracting countries. In such case they enjoy a six month period of priority beginning from the date of filing in the state where the first application was made.

The most interesting provision of this convention is that of Article 9 concerning the remedies of trade mark owners in the contracting countries. This provision constitutes common legislation, and not mere reference to the municipal law of each country. It establishes the means of obtain-

[1] See 19 *Patent and Trade Mark Review* (1921), 337.

ing cancellation of a previously registered mark when on account of such registration the proprietor of such mark does not obtain protection under the convention. In case, for instance, a mark of an American manufacturer or merchant is refused in any of the contracting countries because this mark is already registered by another, he may cause cancellation of such registration by proving any of the following four facts: (1) that he used the mark in the country in question prior to its registration by the other person; (2) that, although he did not use the mark in the country, the registrant had knowledge of the mark's being used by the applicant in other countries; (3) that the registrant had no right to the ownership or use of the mark at the date of its deposit; or (4) that the registered mark is abandoned.

The protection of trade names and indications of origin is also stipulated by the convention. In regard to the former, the provision is taken from Article 8 of the International Convention of 1883. For the protection of the latter, reference is merely made to the domestic law of each country.

Articles 11 of the Convention on Patents and 17 of that on Trade Marks provide that treaties on patents, designs, models, and trade marks previously concluded by and between the signatory states shall be substituted by the new conventions from the date of their ratification as far as the relations between the signatory states are concerned. Thus the Pan American Conventions of 1902 and 1906 are superseded by the new conventions. As regards the Conventions of Montevideo on Patents and on Trade Marks, the latter should be deemed wholly abrogated since three of the four countries, that had ratified it, viz., Peru, Paraguay, and Uruguay, have ratified the convention under consideration. That on patents remains in force as between Peru and Argentina only, which have not ratified the Pan American Convention of 1910.

Of the two Inter-American Bureaus contemplated by the convention, only that of Havana was organized, in 1919,[1] and the first mark was registered on October 28th of that year. Until the year 1923 inclusive, the marks registered and countries from which they originated have been as follows:[2]

Year	*United States of America*	*Cuba*	*Dominican Republic*	*Haiti*
1919.......	80	..	..	..
1920.......	270	15	..	..
1921.......	217	9	..	1
1922.......	173	7	19	2
1923.......	114	7	16	..

3. The Convention of 1923 for the Protection of Trade Marks and Commercial Names

Before the meeting of the Fifth Pan American Conference at Santiago de Chile in March, 1923, the question of Inter-American protection of trade marks formed the subject of study by the Pan American Financial Conference and by the Inter-American High Commission.[3] The Central Executive Council of the latter was assisted in the drafting of a new convention for the protection of trade marks by a number of trade mark experts in the United States.[4] The twenty-one national sections of the Inter-American High Commission were also consulted. But it does not seem that experts

[1] In fact, its organization began on December 6, 1917, when the Cuban Government by a decree of this date decided to establish the Bureau and appointed Dr. Mario Diáz Irizar as its Director. See 24 *Leyes y Decretos de Cuba* (1917), p. 528.

[2] This information was given the present writer by the courtesy of the Director General of the Pan American Union in his letter of June 27, 1928.

[3] See *Preliminary Resolutions for the Consideration of the United States Section of the International High Commission*, Washington, 1915, p. 21; H. R. Doc. 1788, 64th Cong., 2d Sess., p. 21; Sen. Doc. No. 739, 64th Cong., 2d Sess., p. 116; Moore, *The Work of the Inter-American High Commission*, an address delivered at the Pan American Financial Conference, Washington, 1920, p. 6.

[4] See *Convention for the Protection of Commercial, Industrial and Agricultural Trade Marks and Commercial Names* (pamphlet of the Central Executive Council, Inter-American High Commission), Washington, 1923, Introduction.

of Latin American countries gave any assistance in the preparatory work. A draft convention proposed at the Santiago Conference by the United States delegation[1] was adopted and signed by the delegates of all the American countries belonging to the Pan American Union, with the exception of Bolivia, Mexico, and Peru, on April 28, 1923.[2]

The two basic ideas of the revision consisted in the absolute respect of the domestic law of each country and in the satisfaction of the fiscal interest of certain countries which derive income from the registration of marks.[3] The convention entitles to its benefits not all persons, as the convention of 1910, but only "persons domiciled in any of the contracting countries." Consequently, nationals of these countries domiciled in non-contracting countries cannot claim the advantages of the convention. No definition of the commercial, industrial or agricultural trade marks protected by the convention is given therein, as in the convention of 1910.

The Santiago Convention is not a general agreement for the Inter-American protection of trade marks. It corresponds in a certain way to the Madrid arrangement of 1891 of the Industrial Property Union, and has no provisions similar to those of the International Convention of 1883 or of previous Pan American Conventions concerning the national treatment of foreign trade mark owners or a right of priority for filing applications for the registration of trade marks in the contracting countries. Trade mark owners can claim no other protection under this convention except that granted by registration through the Inter-American Bureaus. In

[1] *Report of the Delegates of the United States of America to the Fifth International Conference of American States*, Washington, 1924, p. 17.

[2] See text in English, Spanish, French, and Portuguese in 44 Stat. at L. Pt. 3, p. 2494; also in *United States Treaty Series*, No. 751.

[3] See *Verbatim Record of the Plenary Sessions of the Fifth International Conference of American States*, Santiago de Chile, 1923, Vol. I, p. 325.

case such owners do not wish to apply for registration of their marks through the bureaus, and prefer to acquire protection through direct registration in the countries where they need protection, they are governed exclusively by the municipal law of each country. In such case, they may claim no validation of a trade mark lawfully acquired in their country of origin, as under Article 6 of the International Convention of 1883, nor a right of priority, as under Article 4 of the same convention, not even their assimilation to nationals, as under Article 2 of the same convention. Plainly this is a great defect of the Pan American Convention of 1923, and it does not seem that it has compelled trade mark owners to rush and register their marks through the Inter-American Bureaus, as was probably expected.

The so-called automatic registration in all the contracting countries through registration in one of them is abandoned by this convention. On the other hand, the principle of an international registration at the Inter-American Bureaus as a substitute for registrations in all other American countries, as is the case of the Madrid arrangement of 1891, is not adopted. The necessity of registration in every country in which the proprietor of the trade mark wishes to be protected is maintained. What is then the function of the Inter-American Bureaus? To serve, as the reporter of the draft convention, Mr. Subercaseaux (delegate of Chile), put it, as agents of the manufacturers, merchants or farmers to obtain registration of their marks in any of the contracting countries, or in all of them if they should so desire.[1]

In order to obtain the protection of the convention, the owner of a trade mark must register or deposit it in one of the contracting countries, directly or through duly authorized representatives, and present an application to the respective Inter-American Bureau through the proper office of the

[1] *Ibid.*, p. 326.

country in question, in accordance with the requirements prescribed in the appendix, which forms part of the convention. He must also pay a fee of fifty dollars on each mark for the expenses of the Inter-American Bureaus, plus the fees, charges and expenses provided for by the domestic law of each state in which the applicant desires to be protected.

The administration of the state of first registration or deposit shall send to the Bureau the money order, the electrotype of the mark and a certificate in duplicate containing the data enumerated in Article II of the appendix to the convention. The Bureau, upon receipt of the above, enters them into its books, informs the state of the receipt of the application and of the number and date of entry, and sends copies of the said entry containing all the details to the administration of the states in which the convention has been ratified and in which protection is applied for. The same data shall also be sent to the other contracting states for the purposes of information. Reproductions of the marks received and such particulars as are necessary shall be published in the bulletins of the Inter-American Bureaus.

Upon receipt of an application for registration communicated by the proper Inter-American Bureau, each state shall determine whether protection may be granted in accordance with its laws (Article III). No restriction whatsoever in this respect is imposed on the contracting countries. It should be recalled that under the Madrid arrangement the only grounds for which a mark registered at the Bureau of Berne may be refused protection in any of the contracting countries are those enumerated in Article 6 of the International Convention of 1883.

The decision of each state should be communicated to the Bureau "as soon as possible." Again, the one year limit for such communication, under the Madrid arrangement, does not exist in the convention under consideration.

The notice of acceptance, opposition, or refusal of a mark by the contracting states is to be transmitted by the Bureau to the administration of the state of first registration or deposit with the view of its communication to whom it may concern (Appendix, Art. VI). The Bureau of Berne notifies the administration of the state, as well as the interested party, of the refusal of protection. This secures in favor of the latter a speedier and more certain notification. The intervention of the Inter-American Bureaus serves no more than to obtain for the trade mark owners "in the other signatory states, the same protection granted by them to the marks registered or deposited in their own territory."

However, the advantage of applying through the Inter-American Bureaus consists in the better remedies enjoyed by applicants against the objection of contracting countries to the registration or deposit of a trade mark. These remedies should not necessarily be connected with registration through the bureaus, but they were so provided for in order to compel trade mark owners to make use of the agency of the bureaus. In this respect, Article V, sec. 2, provides:

When refused protection under this convention in a signatory state because of prior registration or a pending application for registration, the proprietor of a mark claiming recognition of rights under this convention shall have the right to seek and obtain the cancellation of the previously registered mark, upon proving, according to the procedure by law of the country where cancellation is sought, such refusal, and either: (*a*) that he had legal protection for his mark in any of the contracting states before the date of application for the registration which he seeks to cancel; or (*b*) that the registrant had no right to the ownership, use or employment of the registered mark at the date of its deposit; or (*c*) that the mark covered by the registration which he seeks to cancel has been abandoned.

The grounds for cancellation (*b*) and (*c*) are taken from Article 9 of the convention of 1910. The ground (*a*) substitutes the grounds of provisions (*a*) and (*b*) of the above article of the previous convention. It is a most important change. While, under the previous convention, the cancellation of a previously registered or deposited mark could only be claimed in case the applicant for cancellation should prove a prior use of the mark within the country where cancellation is sought, or, in case no such use could be proved, knowledge by the registrant of the applicant's use of the mark in another of the contracting countries, under the present convention the legal protection of this mark in any of the contracting countries prior to the application for the registration, the cancellation of which is being sought, is a sufficient ground. By legal protection of the mark is meant a recognition by the law of the ownership of the mark, and not mere protection against imitation by the law of unfair competition. Trade marks enjoy legal protection either after registration or after mere adoption and use. The above provision, then, means that cancellation may be asked if the mark was registered previously by the applicant or if it was used previously by him in any of the contracting countries in which use alone creates ownership of the mark. The good faith of the registrant is immaterial.[1] A critique of this provision is implied in that of the more general provision of Article II, which is dealt with below.

The provision under consideration here applies only when an application for registration through the proper bureau is objected to on the ground that the mark is registered or

[1] The Subcommittee on Trade Mark Protection of the United States Section of the Inter-American High Commission had proposed an amendment of the convention of 1910 in this respect which seemed sound. The grounds for cancellation of a registered or filed mark should be: that an application for Inter-American registration has been filed in the country of origin prior to the date of the application for registration which it is intended to cancel, and that the registrant had knowledge beforehand of the use of the mark in its country of origin. See Pamphlet of the Inter-American High Commission, "*Proposed Revision of the Convention on Trade Marks between the American States of 1910*," p. 5.

filed by another. Nothing is provided for the case where the mark is refused because it resembles closely or may be confused with a mark on the register, or as unlawful according to the domestic law, or by reason of its exterior form. In all such cases the internal law of each country prevails without any limitation.

The grounds of cancellation provided for in sec. 2 of Article V may be claimed by applicants under the convention within a year from the day following that of the receipt by the proper Inter-American Bureau of notice of refusal of protection. But this provision fits ill with that of Article II, where the principle of priority, as will be seen below, is not limited by any period.

No uniform term of protection is enjoyed through registration under the convention, as is the case of the Madrid arrangement. The duration of protection in each state depends on the law of the state (Art. I, Sec. 2). Therefore, the trade marks owners should see that a timely renewal of registration is made in each country, according to the law of each.

The most important effect of registration under the convention is contained in Article II. This article provides:

> The date of filing in the state where first application is made for registration or deposit through the proper Inter-American Bureau, in the absence of other proof of ownership of a mark, shall determine priority for the registration or deposit of such mark in any of the signatory states.

In effect, it would seem that by this provision the automatic registration of the previous convention, thrown out through the front door, is introduced again through the back door. Indeed, registration in only one of the contracting countries is not sufficient to secure protection in the other countries and a registration in the latter is also needed. Yet, by virtue of the above provision, application for regis tration in any of the contracting countries crystallizes the right in the mark for all other countries. The provision amounts to more than a grant of a right of priority for a certain period. For no period is fixed within which such priority may be claimed. The date of the first filing of the mark is only a convenient proof for trade mark owners applying for registration in foreign countries through the Inter-American Bureaus. They may prove, if they can, even an earlier date of ownership of the mark than that shown by the date of filing. Indeed, the article reads ". . . in the absence of other proof of ownership of the mark."

This is especially calculated to benefit American trade mark owners, in view of the fact that in the United States property in a mark is acquired through prior use, and registration in no way determines questions of ownership of the mark, whereas in most of the American countries property in a mark is acquired by registration.[1] By virtue of this provision an American manufacturer who has used a trade mark in the United States or also in other American countries for five years, for instance, without having registered it in any of these countries, may register his mark in the United States and apply for registration or deposit of the same in other American countries through the proper Inter-American Bureau. And in case in the intervening five years another person has registered the same mark, whether in good or in bad faith, the American trade mark owner may cause the annulment of such registration and compel the registration of the mark in his own name.

The provision in this sweeping form is not likely to be assented to by many American countries. It may be theoretically just, but in practice may lead to unjust results. It favors negligent trade mark owners and may cause great

[1] See *infra*, pp. 37 ff.

injury to persons who adopted the same mark in perfectly good faith. In this respect the provisions of the convention of 1910, above considered, were more in accord with real facts and with justice. The public should be given notice of the user's claim in a trade mark. Since neither the mark is used in the country nor the register discloses its adoption by another, a person has no way of knowing of another's claim, and it is unjust to compel him later to give up a valuable asset of his business. It may be assumed with certainty that this provision must have kept many an American country from ratifying the convention.

The provision concerning the protection of commercial names in sec. 4 of the first article is taken from the previous convention and is identical with the provision of Article 8 of the International Convention of 1883.

No material change in the organization of the Bureaus and their duties is introduced by the new convention, except as regards the finances of their service. The two Bureaus of the northern and southern groups of American States are maintained again at Havana and Rio de Janeiro. Colombia and Ecuador, however, are transferred from the southern to the northern group under the present convention, thus leaving six countries in the former against twelve in the latter. The three countries that were not represented at the conference and did not sign the convention of 1923, viz., Mexico, Bolivia, and Peru, are invited to accede to the convention and may be assigned to the group which each may select. Mexico might be expected to select the northern and the other two the southern group.

Although more than a third of the signatory states have ratified the convention, as provided by Article IX, the Bureau in Rio de Janeiro has not begun to function. And in view of the coming Pan American Conference on Trade

Marks, it is believed that its definitive organization may be held in abeyance.[1]

In accordance with Article XIV of the convention, the Government of Chile has notified the contracting countries that the convention of 1923, having been ratified by the United States of America, the United States of Brazil, Cuba, Paraguay, Haiti, and the Dominican Republic,[2] went into effect on September 30, 1926.[3] Chile also ratified it on the latter date, and Guatemala on April 23, 1925. According to the same article, as far as the relations of these countries are concerned, the convention of 1910 ceased to be in effect.

Thus, at the present time, the net result of the Pan American Conventions on industrial property is the following:

(1) The Montevideo Convention of 1889 on Trade Marks has been abrogated.

(2) The Montevideo Convention of 1889 on Patents remains in effect only as between Argentina and Peru.

(3) The Pan American Convention of Mexico City (1902) on Patents, Industrial Drawings, Models and Trade Marks, and the Pan American Convention of Rio de Janeiro (1906) have been abrogated.

(4) The Pan American Convention of 1910 relating to Patents and Industrial Designs and Models is in effect as between thirteen American countries, viz., Brazil, Costa Rica, Cuba, the Dominican Republic, Ecuador, Guatemala, Haiti, Honduras, Nicaragua, Panama, Paraguay, the United States, and Uruguay.

[1] According to information given the present writer by the Director General of the Pan American Union, letter dated June 25, 1928.

[2] The dates of ratification are as follows: Brazil, January 12, 1924; Cuba, August 2, 1924; the Dominican Republic, October 7, 1925; Haiti, June 22, 1925; Paraguay, May 26, 1924; and the United States, February 24, 1925. (According to information given the present writer by the Director General of the Pan American Union, letter dated July 26, 1928.)

[3] See Proclamation by the President of the United States in 44 Stat. at L. Pt. 3, p. 2526.

(5) The Pan American Convention of 1910 concerning the protection of Trade Marks is in effect as between Ecuador, Panama, Peru, and Uruguay, which have ratified the convention of 1910, but not that of 1923, and as between each of these countries and the other six countries that had ratified the convention of 1910, viz., Brazil, Cuba, the Dominican Republic, Haiti, Paraguay, and the United States.

(6) The Pan American Convention of 1923 concerning the protection of Commercial, Industrial and Agricultural Trade Marks and Commercial Names is in effect as between eight American countries, viz., Brazil, Chile, Cuba, the Dominican Republic, Guatemala, Haiti, Paraguay, and the United States.

On the other hand, the business of the Inter-American Bureau at Havana has receded in the meantime instead of progressing. The registrations, which had fallen from 270 for the United States in 1920 to 114 in 1923, and from 15 to 7 for Cuba, were as follows in the next years:[1]

Year	*United States of America*	*Cuba*	*Dominican Republic*	*Haiti*
1924........	83	15	8	..
1925........	60	7	3	..
1926........	100	6	..	..
1927.......	34	4	1	..

4. Resolution of the Conference of Havana

The revision of the Trade Marks Conventions of 1910 and 1923 was on the agenda of the Sixth International Conference of American States which was called together at Havana on January 16, 1928. In a report submitted to the sixth committee of this conference by the delegate of Argentina, Mr. Espil, the failure of the five previous conferences to arrive at uniform rules of protection of trade marks was inquired into. This delegate was of the opinion

[1] According to information given the present writer by the courtesy of the Director General of the Pan American Union, letter dated June 27, 1928.

that the failure was due to the lack of desire on the part of many American countries to ratify instruments which it was felt were adopted without careful and conscientious study, taking into account all the national interests involved. Mr. Espil thought that the matter of dealing with such matters of extreme legal and technical specialization was not that of diplomatic conferences, as was done hitherto, but by holding conferences of specialists, as was done in Europe in the case of the Industrial Property Union. He concluded that the failure of the attempts to establish an Inter-American system of protection of industrial property should make the American States think that perhaps the solution may lie in their accession to the Convention of Paris and the Madrid Arrangement. More outspoken in this respect was the Mexican delegate, who declared that the Mexican Government has maintained with absolute firmness its attitude of being a member of the universal Industrial Property Union and of refusing accession to the Pan American Conventions.[1]

On the proposition of the delegation of Argentina, the committee adopted a resolution recommending to the Governing Board of the Pan American Union "the calling of a special conference of representatives of the Union, to be held at such place and date as it may designate, for the purpose of studying in its amplest scope the problem of the Inter-American protection of trade marks." The conclusions of this Conference are to be forwarded through the medium of the Pan American Union for the consideration of the different governments without the need of a further reference to the Seventh International Conference of American States.

The conference of specialists was called together at Washington for February 11, 1929.

[1] See *Documentary Information by the Pan American Union relative to the Pan American Trade Mark Conference*, Washington, 1928, pp. 3, 19.

III

PROBLEMS IN THE INTER-AMERICAN PROTECTION OF BUSINESS RELATIONS

1. The Interests of the Various American Countries

THE efforts of two score years on the part of the American countries for arriving at a conventional regime for the protection of trade marks and trade names aimed ultimately at the protection of the foreign trade of these countries and of advantageous business relations created or maintained by business organizations. No creation of special privileges or exchange of favors between the contracting countries was embodied in the conventions which were adopted since 1889. By the protection of trade marks, trade names, and other distinctive badges used by manufacturers or traders to create, maintain and extend the good will of their business, the freedom of honest commerce and industry is in no way curtailed. The prohibition of their infringement and imitation by business parasites is in no way different from the prohibition of stealing another's property. The protection of business relations serves not only the interests of business men but also of the purchasing public against deceit and fraud. In the last resort, therefore, it is the social interest of preventing dishonest and unfair competition and of furthering fair dealing which is at stake and which is the policy of any country to secure.

A clear vision of these facts and of the interests which are to be protected is needed for a proper understanding of the problems presented in the Inter-American regime of trade marks, trade names, etc. It is of no use to conceal the fact that international protection of business relations in the American countries means, to a large degree, the protection of such relations of nationals of the United States in Latin America. It is an indisputable fact that at the present time the United States, a highly industrialized country, is in a different position, so far as the protection of foreign trade is concerned, from the Latin American countries which produce and export only raw materials. The latter countries rarely register any trade marks in the United States Patent Office and the problem of protection of their trade marks, trade names, etc. in the United States is hardly existing. On the contrary, the export trade of the United States in these countries in the last fifteen years took a rapid and great development. The protection of this trade through the protection of trade marks, trade names and other distinctive signs against infringement and imitation is a vital question for American manufacturers and traders.

This does not mean, however, that any convention for the protection of trade marks and repression of unfair competition is a one-sided affair, aiming exclusively at the protection of interests of the nationals of the United States. Assuredly, by the infringement and imitation of American trade marks, the interests of American manufacturers and traders are injured. But this is only the one side of the picture, and a short-sided view of things. Indeed, the primary purpose of the imitation of a trade mark or trade name or of the commission of any act of unfair competition is to deceive the purchasing public as to the maker or seller of goods and to sell to such public goods of inferior quality under the guise of a trade mark or other distinctive sign identified with a well-known quality or kind of goods.

Besides, trade marks of nationals of the United States are infringed upon and imitated in Latin American countries not only by nationals of these countries but also by American nationals domiciled or possessing commercial or industrial establishments in these countries, as the present writer has been informed by trade mark attorneys in this country.

The impunity, therefore, enjoyed in Latin America by persons injuring advantageous business relations of American manufacturers or traders, while prejudicial to the latter, is more profoundly harmful to the interests of Latin American countries. Frauds are being permitted against the purchasing public in favor of a small number of business parasites, sometimes foreigners who use the land in which they are established for the commission of acts which, if they are not punishable under the existing laws, are contrary to any rule of commercial loyalty and to the general policy of every state to secure the social interest of fair dealing in commercial and industrial transactions. Any unfair practice in this respect permeates in the long run and injures the whole legal order of the country which tolerates it.

On the other hand, the lack of an adequate protection of business relations of foreign manufacturers and traders in the American countries is harmful in another respect. There are nascent industries at the present time in many Latin American countries and their development may best be stimulated by the protection of foreign business relations, which puts a premium upon the improvement of national production. To quote the German Patent Office in a decision protecting a French appellation for cheese against infringement by a German trade mark, "the most efficacious means of protecting and developing national production is not to contribute to the development and amelioration of foreign reputed products by the use of their appellations, but by bettering the quality of national products."[1]

[1] See decision of January 21, 1919, concerning the mark "Hoefelmayrs Silber Camembert" in *Blatt für Patent- Muster- und Zeichenwesen*, 1919, p. 11.

2. The Question of Registration Through Inter-American Bureaus

If the problem of protection of trade marks and trade names and of repression of acts of unfair competition seems, thus, to interest all the American countries, the question of registration of trade marks through the Inter-American Bureaus does not appeal equally to those countries. The history of registrations from 1919 at the Bureau in Havana shows that the only countries which availed themselves of the privilege of registering trade marks through the Bureau are: the United States, Cuba, the Dominican Republic, and Haiti. From a total of 1254 registrations in the nine years ending in 1927, 1131 trade marks were transmitted to the Bureau from the United States, 70 from Cuba, 47 from the Dominican Republic and 3 from Haiti.

From the Argentine Delegate, Mr. Espil's, report at the Sixth International Conference in Havana it would appear that several American countries base their unwillingness to ratify the Conventions on Trade Marks of 1910 and 1923 on the institution of the Inter-American Bureaus. It was a fatal defect of those Conventions that they failed to distinguish the two problems of trade mark registration and trade mark protection and made the latter conditional on registration through the Inter-American Bureaus.

Besides, it is doubtful whether the question of registration through these Bureaus is of any interest to American trade mark owners. The latter prefer and are advised to apply direct in the various American countries for the registration of their marks, which assures them of speedy registration and defense against oppositions. Moreover, most of the American trade marks actually in use in export trade in Latin America are already registered. What American manufacturers and traders, therefore, need especially today is not a less expensive and centralized registration of trade marks but a more effective and complete protection of existing trade mark rights.

3. The Problem of Protection of Priority of Trade Marks

When the question of Inter-American protection of business relations is thus cleared of the above difficulties and is placed on the right plane, it is possible to put a finger on the real problems of the situation. Indeed, these are mainly two and spring out of the following state of things.

An American manufacturer or trader may use a trade mark in connection with export trade in American countries. His trade mark may or may not have been registered in the country where he is domiciled or possesses his industrial or commercial establishment. In certain American countries and primarily in the United States a trade mark is protected by the law by reason of its mere adoption and use by the manufacturer in question. Suppose that this manufacturer uses his trade mark in the United States, Cuba, and Brazil for many years and later wishes to import his products into Argentina. He runs two risks. First, if he neglects to register his mark in Cuba and Brazil as soon as he establishes business relations in these countries, another may register the same mark or a mark so closely resembling his own that a confusion may be produced. As a result, the registrant of this mark will seek to absorb by deception of patrons the unearned benefit of another's activity and money. Secondly, when the latter, through the extension of his business to Argentina, imports his products in that country, he may find that his mark is already registered there by a third person and his products may be liable to seizure and forfeiture. The Argentine registrant may have registered that mark in good faith, unaware of the first person's use of the same mark, or in bad faith, with knowledge of such prior use.

This is the first problem. It may be defined as *the problem of protecting the priority of trade marks.*

4. The Problem of Effective Protection Against Infringement and Unfair Competition

Another situation is this. An American trade mark owner may have registered his mark in all the American countries to protect his business relations in every one of them. Third persons in some of these countries may attempt to register imitation marks or counterfeit his trade mark, or, without infringing upon the trade mark, may imitate the form of the container of the products or the wrapping, labels or get-up of such products. In all such cases the effect is always the same. The customers of the trade mark owner are deceived by the appearance of the third person's goods and the business relations of the former are injured. The same effect is produced when the trade name or an indication of place of origin of a manufacturer is misappropriated or imitated. The trade mark owner must be able to protect his trade against such acts and dealings and not be the easy victim of such business parasites. A legal protection cannot be of real benefit unless it may be applied speedily and effectively. A civil suit for damages alone which may take a number of years before its termination is really a denial of protection.

This is the second problem. It may be defined as *the problem of effective protection against infringement and unfair competition.*

It may, indeed, be said that a Convention between the American countries for the protection of trade marks, trade names, etc., will not really amount to anything, unless it tackles these two problems and attempts to solve them as completely as possible.

IV.

DIFFICULTIES OF INTERNATIONAL REGULATION

1. Protection of Priority of Trade Marks

THE first of the above described two problems is the more difficult to solve. The impossibility to find a proper solution of this problem as much as the institution of registration through the Inter-American Bureaus have been the stumbling-blocks to the ratification of the previous Pan American Conventions by all the American countries. The delegates of the United States are perhaps more to be blamed for this failure than those of Latin American countries, because they have not taken sufficient account of the public policy underlying the law of those countries.

One must keep in mind the three systems of trade mark registration in American countries and try to understand the theories and considerations underlying these systems.

(*a*) *First System. Ownership Based on Priority of Use.*

It is generally admitted that a trade mark cannot be understood apart from a business the products of which it serves to distinguish and individualize. Its value springs from adoption and use by a manufacturer or trader. The law everywhere, in protecting a trade mark, does not protect the material sign or mark itself as a creation or invention of the user, but the value that the use of that sign or mark in connection with the user's business has for the latter. This explains the fact that until fifty years ago the right in a trade mark was everywhere acquired by prior adoption and use, registration being only declaratory of property in a trade mark. The registrant of a trade mark was only prima facie owner; anyone could show a prior use and cause the cancellation of the registration. This is true no longer. Comparatively in few countries registration of a trade mark is simply declaratory of property therein.

Outside the United States, four other American countries: Colombia, Ecuador, Honduras, and Nicaragua, retain this old system of law, according to which property in a trade mark is acquired by adoption and use and registration is only declaratory of the right.[1] At the present time there is a vigorous movement under way in the United States for making compulsory the registration of trade marks used in commerce among the several States or with foreign countries,[2] as the existing state of law is not considered satisfactory.[3]

(*b*) *Second System. Ownership Based on Priority of Registration.*

The recent legislation in other countries is explained by modern commercial conditions in the world. The market of any given industrial or commercial concern is no longer limited within definite boundaries. The facilities of communication and transportation and all the other equipment of the business world extend the possibilities of markets of any sort of goods. An industry or trade may start with a market limited on a small part of a country's territory, then extend it to the whole territory of a country and later to any number of foreign countries.

[1] Similar is the law in this respect in Canada, Finland, Italy, Luxemburg, the Netherlands, Rumania, Switzerland, and Turkey. Also in France and Tunis. But in France there is a great movement for the change of the law in this respect. In the French protectorate Morocco already the law is changed. And in the mandated territory of Syria and Lebanon the French Government introduced a law following the principles of the British Law in this respect.

[2] Ed. S. Rogers. *Some Suggestions concerning a Trade Mark Registration Act* in (1920) 45 *Reports of the American Bar Association* 421–422.

[3] See Hearings before the Committee on Patents, 69th Cong., 1st Sess. (1926) H. R. 6248, pp. 38 ff. and 2d Sess. (1927) H. R. 13486, pp. 14 ff.

If only the national territory be considered, the possibility of the extension of the market of a business over the whole territory of a country raises the question of protection of a trade mark of that business in all such territory and not on that part alone to which the business extends and on which its products are found for the time being. But then the public should be given notice of the user's claim in a trade mark. As the latter is not used in all the territory at the same time and notice by the use alone is not available, another kind of notice should be given. This is afforded by the registration of trade marks. Manufacturers or traders may consult the register of trade marks and avoid adopting a mark which is already adopted and used by another. Thus, conflicts between bona fide users of the same mark are avoided. Thus, prior adoption and use of the mark in the whole territory of a country is predicated upon the registration of a trade mark. The person who first adopts and uses a mark is required to register it; unless he does so, he cannot complain against any one else's registering in good faith the same mark. He failed to give notice of his claim to the public which cannot be blamed for ignoring it. When this is the condition of things, the law may well prescribe that by registration of a trade mark property therein is acquired.

These are the considerations and the policy underlying the law of twelve Latin American countries in which ownership in a trade mark is acquired by registration. These countries are Argentina, Bolivia, Chile, Costa Rica, Cuba, Dominican Republic, Guatemala, Haiti, Panama, Paraguay, Peru, and Venezuela.[1]

These two systems are in complete opposition. From the point of view of international protection, this opposition

[1] Similar is the law in this respect in China, Danzig, Germany, Greece, Japan, Norway, Poland, and Sweden.

may lead to a perfectly valid registration and, possibly usurpation of American trade marks by third persons in the above twelve countries. And the question is whether we may respect the independence of the municipal law of each country and yet protect vested rights in trade marks and business reputations.

(*c*) *Third System. Ownership Based on Uncontested Registration for a Specified Period.*

In this respect the third system of trade mark registration prevailing in four American countries: Brazil, Mexico, Salvador, and Uruguay as well as in most of the countries of the world,[1] may afford a basis for working out a solution admissible to all parties. This system is determined by the following considerations. A manufacturer or trader may have good reasons for neglecting to register a trade mark as soon as he adopts and uses it. He may use several marks in connection with his business and may not realize immediately their psychological value from a business point of view. A trade mark may sometimes be forced upon the producer by the public. When such a fortuitous and unintentional sign becomes valuable, the person using it may consider registering and protecting it from imitators. But by that time another may have registered the same mark. Should the latter prevail always and the prior user be compelled to give up a valuable element of the good will of his business? The system of the above twelve American countries, according to which property in a trade mark is based

[1] This is the system of the law of Great Britain and of many British Dominions and Colonies (including the Irish Free State, Commonwealth of Australia, New Zealand, and Ceylon), also of Austria, Bulgaria, Czechoslovakia, Denmark, Esthonia, Hungary, Morocco, Portugal, Serb-Croat-Slovene State, Spain, Syria and Lebanon, and U. S. S. R.

The law of Mexico followed the previous system until recently. The new régime is effective from January 1, 1919.

on priority of registration, may result in great injustices and abuses.

The system of the laws of Brazil, Mexico, Salvador, and Uruguay and of the other countries of the world is calculated to afford a remedy thereto. The law provides that registration of a trade mark serves only to declare the ownership for a period of years. Within this period the manufacturer or trader who first used such mark may prove such prior use and cause the cancellation of registration. The registrant is only a *prima facie* owner of the mark. At the lapse of such period, however, the right of the registrant becomes conclusive. No proof of prior use is allowed and the registration cannot be cancelled, unless obtained by fraud.

This system of trade mark registration is of a very recent development. In 1883, when the Industrial Property Union was created, only two countries had this system: Great Britain and Portugal. It is interesting to note that in the French protectorate Morocco and the mandated territory of Syria and Lebanon this modern legislation represents a change from the traditional French régime of priority of use as the sole basis of ownership in trade marks. This system was also recommended by the Congress of the International Association for the Protection of Industrial Property as model for the uniformity of the law of the various countries.[1]

The period from registration at the expiry of which the registrant's right becomes conclusive is five years in Brazil and Salvador, three years in Mexico, and two years in Uruguay. In the other countries of the world where the

[1] See *Annuaire* of the Association, 1900, pp. 197, 348, 466 and 496. The eminent French writer Eugène Pouillet, positively hostile to this system for a long time, was converted to it "by its manifest advantages"; see *ibid.*, p. 351.

See also the same view by the president of the French Association for the protection of industrial property in *Travaux du Groupe Français de l'Association Internationale*, 1919–1923, pp. 44–46.

same system prevails the period varies from seven years (Great Britain, Australia, Irish Free State, New Zealand) to six months (Portugal). In most of these countries the conclusiveness of the registrant's right is subject to the sanctions for non-user of the registered mark. Also registration may be cancelled even after the specified period has expired if obtained by fraud,[1] or if proved that at the time of registration the mark in question was considered in the interested commercial circles as the distinctive sign of the plaintiff's products.[2]

(d) The Application of a Regime Analogous to the Third System in the International Legal Order.

It is submitted that a régime analogous to this third system on the legal effects of trade mark registration should govern the international protection of trade marks in the American countries. In other words, the registrant's right in a trade mark registered in any American country should not be considered conclusive as regards the persons domiciled or possessing business establishments in the other contracting countries until the expiry of a certain period from such registration.

This is, in effect, the regime of trade marks in the Industrial Property Union constituted by the International Convention of 1883–1925.

The right of priority enjoyed under Article 4 of this Convention by the persons entitled to its benefits makes it possible for the manufacturer or trader who files for registration a trade mark in one of the contracting countries to apply for its registration in all the other countries within a period of six months. If in the interval the same trade mark or one infringing it has been registered in the name of another

[1] This is so in Great Britain, Australia, Irish Free State, New Zealand, Morocco, and Syria and Lebanon.

[2] This is so in Austria, Czechoslovakia, and Hungary.

person, it may be taken off the register at the request of the applicant. This means that the registrant's right in a trade mark in any of the contracting countries may become conclusive as regards persons who have filed the same mark in another of the contracting countries only at the expiry of a six month period from the date of such filing.

As is clear, this provision is insufficient for the solution of the problem of protection of priority of trade marks in the American countries, for two reasons. It benefits only marks which are filed for registration; and the six month period is too short. In the United States, because of the legal protection enjoyed by non-registered marks, many trade marks are not registered. On the other hand, many American countries are separated by great distances and little use may be made of the six month period of priority.

In the Industrial Property Union itself the priority of trade marks is protected by another provision. This is the new article 6bis adopted at the Conference of The Hague, which met in October 1925 for the purpose of revising the International Convention of 1883–1911. According to this article, a trade mark owner may obtain the cancellation of the registration of his trade mark or of an imitation mark by another person in any of the contracting countries when the mark is proved to be well-known in that country as being already his mark. This right for claiming the removal of the mark may be exercised within three years from the registration of the mark or at any time when the registration was made in bad faith.

As is seen, this provision does not tend only to protect marks filed for registration in the country of origin, but any trade mark used by a manufacturer or trader in the contracting countries. Moreover, the period is of three years in case of bona fide registrations and unlimited in case of fraudulent registrations. Thus, in effect, the registrant's right in any of the thirty-eight countries of the Industrial Property Union is not conclusive until the lapse of at least three years from registration. This is so only as regards trade marks which are considered by the competent authority of the country of registration to be well-known in that country as being already the marks of *ressortissants* of another contracting country and utilized for the same or similar classes of goods. This is the only limitation. It is not sufficient, therefore, to prove prior use of the mark in any other country, but the country of registration. Nor is it sufficient to prove a casual and rare use of the mark in the country in question. It is necessary that the interested circles in that country know that the mark belongs to the complaining party.

The above two provisions of the International Convention seem to have instituted, in effect, in the relations between the member countries of the Industrial Property Union, an international régime analogous to the previously described third system of trade mark registration. They should aid in solving the problem of priority of trade marks in the Inter-American régime.

2. Protection Against Infringement and Unfair Competition

This problem is twofold. On the one hand, it raises the question of effective remedies against acts of infringement of trade marks, trade names and other distinctive signs used by manufacturers and traders for their business relations. On the other, it demands a broad conception of unfair competition.

(*a*) *Effective Remedies Against Infringement.*

The kind and quality of remedies afforded in each country in case of infringement of the above rights is so much in the province of municipal law that little can be done through a convention. It is impossible to adopt provisions in this respect to be applied uniformly in the various contracting countries, unless one is prepared to make uniform the law of procedure, the civil law, and the criminal law in the various countries. Any stipulation on remedies tending to affect the municipal law of the various countries should necessarily leave much scope for the traditional technique and practice and the general law of each country. In this way the independence of the law of each country would be respected and the needs of international life would be satisfied.

The International Convention of 1883–1925 solved the difficulties in this respect as follows: By its article 2 it provides that the persons entitled to its benefits shall enjoy the remedies and protection afforded by the law of each country to its nationals. However, in article 9, certain specific remedies are provided for which are calculated to afford a speedy and effective protection in infringement cases. These remedies are: (*a*) seizure on importation of goods bearing illegally a trade mark or trade name; (*b*) prohibition of importation of such goods; and (*c*) seizure within the country. The same remedies are extended to the repression of false indications of origin. The effect of this provision is the following: In case the law of a member country contains provisions for the prohibition of importation or seizure of goods, such provisions must necessarily be applied in favor of persons entitled to the benefits of the Convention. But a country is not bound to grant by legislation the above remedies. Indeed, the last paragraph of article 9 provides that the above remedies, pending modification of the municipal law, shall be replaced by the remedies available in such cases to nationals.

In fact, these provisions of article 9 have affected indirectly the municipal law of the member countries of the Industrial Property Union. They held out a desideratum to which the law of these countries tended to conform. Eighteen countries of the Union[1] now possess legislation providing for the administrative seizure on importation or prohibition of articles bearing infringing marks. In eight the judicial seizure within the country may be applied for[2]; and in five countries both the seizure on importation and the seizure within the country are possible.[3]

Moreover, by a new article 10ter adopted at the Conference of The Hague, 1925, the contracting countries undertake to assure to persons entitled to the benefits of the Convention appropriate legal remedies to repress effectively all acts of infringement and unfair competition. Penal sanctions and injunctions against the continuance of infringement acts would seem to have been understood by the Conference of The Hague as the remedies referred to in the engagement of article 10ter.[4]

(b) *Repression of Unfair Competition.*

Trade marks and trade names are not the only devices and distinctive badges used by a manufacturer or trader for maintaining and extending the good will and reputation of his business, nor is their infringement or imitation the only means of injuring the business relations of a person. The technical trade mark law, therefore, of the American countries and the treaty stipulations for the protection of trade marks and trade names are not sufficient for the protection of advantageous business relations of manufacturers or traders of the contracting countries. Fraudulent persons often

[1] Brazil, Bulgaria, Cuba, Czechoslovakia, Dominican Republic, Finland, France, Germany, Great Britain, Hungary, Portugal, Spain, Switzerland, Tunis, and the United States.

[2] Austria, Greece, Italy, Morocco, Mexico, Rumania, Syria and Lebanon, and Turkey.

[3] France, Hungary, Portugal, Switzerland, and Tunis.

[4] See *Actes de la Conférence de La Haye de l'Union pour la Protection de la Propriété Industrielle*, Berne, 1926, pp. 478–479.

attempt to steal the business of successful producers by keeping outside the limits of trade mark law. For instance, they do not copy or counterfeit the trade mark or trade name of another, but they imitate the form of the container of another's product, the wrapping, labels or other distinctive signs.

It is an undeniable fact of modern business life that successful manufacturers or traders have to cope with the danger of having the good will of their business, their connection with the purchasing public, interfered with by unscrupulous competitors. This is a fact in all countries of the world. It is especially important to foreigners. Their absence from a country where their products possess a market, their inability to act with speediness and prevent the deception of their patrons puts a premium on the commission of acts of unfair competition against them.

In various civil law countries such acts against the commercial loyalty in industrial and commercial transactions were reached by application of general principles of law. The decisions of the courts in this respect reflected the reactions of public opinion in trade. In the Common Law countries the most adequate remedy of equitable injunction was applied more and more freely to all cases where a person attempted to pass off his goods as those of another. In other countries, on the contrary (for instance in Germany), the courts have not shown an adequate power of adaptability and have been unsuccessful at protecting against unfair competition. In the Latin American countries the legal materials at hand did not afford sufficient elasticity.

(*c*) *Recent Development of the Law of Unfair Competition.*

In recent years a great development of the law of unfair competition has been accomplished. In all the countries earnest efforts are being made to protect the business relations of competing manufacturers or traders without destroying competition, and to defeat the frauds committed by business parasites. In an increasing number of countries, it was found that commercial affairs moved and changed too rapidly to await the slow process of the growth of law by court decisions through experience and development by logical deduction, and that the interests clamoring for protection should be satisfied by special legislation reaching all known and foreseen acts of unfair competition. This is also, perhaps, one of the phases of the general faith in the efficacy of conscious effort to improve law and to improve society through law, which constitutes one of the chief characteristics of twentieth century legal history.[1]

Germany took the lead in this direction with the Acts of 1894 and 1896 which are superseded now by the Act of June 7, 1909,[2] a most excellent piece of legislative work. A general principle in its first article proclaims that a petition for injunction and an action for damages may be brought against any person who, for the purpose of competition, commits in business acts contrary to honest practices. Following this general principle, various acts of unfair competition are specified and prohibited, such as, deceptive and unfair advertising, selling below a fixed price under certain conditions, interference with contracts with servants, discrediting the goods, the person, or the business establishment of a third party, acts causing confusion with the name, firm, or trade name of another, and misuse of business or trade secrets. Whenever such acts are accomplished with bad faith, criminal sanctions are also imposed. For an in-

[1] On the present law of unfair competition in the various countries see an excellent research published in the review *Gesetzgebung und Rechtspraxis des Auslandes* in a series of articles in 1926, 1927 and 1928. These articles are reproduced in French in the periodical published by the Berne Bureau of the Industrial Property Union "*La Propriété Industrielle*," 1928, pp. 38 ff., 60 ff., 81 ff., 110 ff., and 137 ff.

[2] *Gesetz gegen den unlauteren Wettbewerb* in *Reichsgesetzblatt*, 1909, p. 499.

junction against most of these acts suit may be brought by professional associations constituted for the protection of industrial interests.

The substance of the German Act was adopted in Greece (1914), Austria (1923), Hungary (1923), Latvia (1927), and Czechoslovakia (1927).[1] Similar enactments reaching various acts of unfair competition were made in Denmark, Sweden, Turkey, and Norway.[2] The Spanish Act on Industrial Property of 1902 contains provisions against unfair competition.[3] The Colombian Law of December 10, 1914,[4] in articles 51 and 52, provides that a petition for injunction and an action for damages may be brought for all acts of unfair competition. But the definition of unfair competition of article 51 is somewhat narrow. The Polish Law of August 2, 1926 is tackling the question of unfair competition in the most complete way by recognizing a property right in a business enterprise and the attractive force or good will of such enterprise and prohibiting all acts of misappropriation or injury to such property right.[5]

[1] Greece, "*Κώδηξ τῆς Θέμιδος*" 1914, p. 34. This law was amended by the laws of June 6, 1926 and November 12, 1927. ("*Ἐφημερίς τῆς Κυβερνήσεως*", 1926, p. 1628, and 1927, p. 1819).

Austria, Act No. 531 of September 26, 1923 (*Bundesgesetzblatt*, 1923. II. 1717).

Hungary, Act No. 6 of 1923 (*Ungarische Reichsgesetzsammlung*, 1923, p. 31).

Latvia, Act of October 4, 1927 (*Propriété Industrielle*, 1928, p. 105).

Czechoslovakia, Act of July 15, 1927 (*Propriété Industrielle*, 1928, p. 131).

[2] Denmark, the previous Acts of 1918 and 1921 were superseded by the Act No. 98 of March 29, 1924, modified by the Act No. 107 of April 9, 1926 (*Lovtidende for Danmark*, 1924, p. 603; and 1926, p. 589).

Sweden, Act No. 446 of June 19, 1919 (*Svensk Förfatningssamling*, 1919, II. p. 1009).

Turkey, Articles 56–65 of the new Turkish Commercial Code (*Propriété Industrielle*, 1928, p. 141).

Norway, Law No. 11 of July 7, 1922 (*Norsk Lovtidende* 1922, p. 287), amended by the Act of March 12, 1926 (*Propriété Industrielle*, 1927, p. 193).

[3] Act of May 16, 1902 (*Boletin de Legislación*, 1902, II. p. 88). See also Decree of November 28, 1925 (*Ibid.*, 1925, VI. p. 440).

[4] *Leyes de Colombia*, 1914, p. 237.

[5] See this law in *La Propriété Industrielle*, 1927, p. 8 and an article by Professor Zoll explaining the principles of this law, *ibid.*, pp. 64 ff.

(*d*) *The Provisions of the International Convention of 1883–1925.*

While the law of unfair competition was undergoing this development in the municipal legal order of the various countries a similar evolution was being made in the international legal order established by the International Convention of Paris. In 1900 a provision was inserted in this Convention as article 10bis to the effect that the persons entitled to its benefits shall enjoy in each of the contracting countries the protection afforded nationals against acts of unfair competition. In 1911 this provision was revised. It was provided that the contracting countries are bound to assure to the above persons an effective protection against unfair competition. Lastly, in 1925, this provision was further amended by the addition of two new paragraphs. The one contains a definition of unfair competition. Every act of competition contrary to honest practices in industrial or commercial matters is declared to constitute an act of unfair competition. The other paragraph enumerates certain acts of unfair competition which must be repressed in each of the contracting countries. These are: acts creating confusion with the goods of a competitor, and false allegations, in the course of trade, of such a nature as to discredit the goods of a competitor.

This provision leaves this much to be desired, that it contains no immediate sanction. If a country has no well-established law of unfair competition either in the form of a body of court decisions or in the form of a special Act, as those enumerated above, no real protection may be enjoyed by nationals of other countries by virtue of the stipulation of article 10bis alone. It should be possible for persons entitled to the benefits of the Convention to claim in such case the application of the provisions of the trade mark law on infringement of trade marks against acts of unfair competition.[1]

The stipulation of article 10bis of the International Convention of 1883, amended as proposed above, would seem to afford a way of solving the difficulties presented by unfair competition in the relations between the American countries. But it may also be inquired whether it would not be possible to discuss and adopt a model of unfair competition law to be enacted by those of the American countries where there exists no law of unfair competition or where the existing law has not been able to keep pace with the protean transformations of fraud in commercial transactions. In such case the above enactments of various European countries may be availed of with profit.

[1] Such a provision exists in the Madrid Arrangement of 1891 for the Repression of False Indications of Origin, entered into by fourteen of the member countries of the Industrial Property Union. (See last paragraph of article 1 of that Arrangement).

V

SUGGESTIONS FOR THE COMING PAN AMERICAN TRADE MARK CONFERENCE

THE special Conference of representatives of American countries "for the purpose of studying in its amplest scope the problem of the Inter-American protection of trade marks" will meet at Washington on February 11, 1929. The calling of this conference of specialists on a subject of great technicality needing long and careful study constitutes a felicitous departure from the previous practice of drafting such conventions by the general Pan American Conferences. The success of this Conference will depend on its desire to tackle all the problems of the Inter-American régime of trade marks and unfair competition and to eliminate the stumbling-blocks to the ratification of previous Conventions on this subject. Inasmuch as there has not been a long preparation and continuity of study of these questions in all the American countries, it is reasonable to make use of the experience acquired by other countries in dealing with the same problems.

The widest and longest experience in this respect is afforded by the International Union for the protection of industrial property. Its various provisions in relation to the problems of international protection of trade marks and of repression of unfair competition were considered in the preceding chapter. The question of a centralized registration of trade marks was solved in the Industrial Property Union at a very early date in the right way. The Madrid Trade Mark Arrangement of 1891 entered into by many of the members of the general Union provides for the registration of trade marks at the Berne Bureau of the Union and for transmission of such marks to the countries parties to the Arrangement.

After repeated failures in the Pan American Union, one is forced to realize that the same distinction between a general convention for the protection of trade marks and the repression of unfair competition and a special Arrangement for the Inter-American registration and transmission of trade marks to such countries as will enter into and ratify such Arrangement, is the only solution imposed. In the opposite course, the destinies of the Pan American Convention and the important advantages it purports to afford would be staked on a matter of such small practical value as the institution of the Inter-American Bureaus.[1]

It follows that, in the present writer's opinion, the "Draft of Convention on the Inter-American protection of trade marks," prepared by a special committee of the Governing Board of the Pan American Union, does not seem adequate for the solution of the problems of Inter-American regulation of trade marks. For it does not remove the two main objections of Latin American countries to the previous Pan American conventions: the necessity of subscribing to the institution of the Inter-American registration of marks by adopting and ratifying the convention, and the substitution of their own conception of trade mark priority by a régime which is virtually that of the law of the United States. A conventional régime cannot be established when a country attempts to impose upon the other contracting countries its own law, but when the laws of the various countries are harmonized with a view of meeting the demands of international life.

One would suppose that the best solution of the Inter-American problems of protection of trade marks as well as of other rights of industrial property would be the accession

[1] See *supra*, pp. 34 ff.

of all the American Republics to the Industrial Property Union, as the Mexican and Argentine delegations repeatedly urged at the Conferences of American States. It would seem, however, that several American Republics are not interested in joining that Union. And the next best thing is to make use of the experience of the Industrial Property Union in solving the problems of Inter-American protection.

In accordance with the above exposition, it is submitted that the coming Pan American Trade Mark Conference should consider, discuss and adopt the following international acts:

A. Draft of a Convention for the Protection of Trade Marks, Trade Names and Indications of Place of Origin and for the Repression of Unfair Competition

ARTICLE 1.

The contracting countries constitute themselves into a Union for the protection of trade marks, trade names, and indications of origin and for the repression of unfair competition.

ARTICLE 2.

Persons domiciled or who have real or effective industrial or commercial establishments in any of the contracting countries shall, as regards the protection of their trade marks, trade names, and indications of place of origin and the repression of unfair competition, enjoy in all the other countries of the Union the advantages that the respective laws now grant or may hereafter grant to their nationals, without prejudice to the rights specially provided by the present convention. Consequently, they shall have the same protection as the latter, and the same legal remedies against any infringement of their rights, provided they observe the conditions and formalities imposed on nationals.

ARTICLE 3.

Every trade mark legally protected in any of the contracting countries shall be admitted for deposit and protected in its original form in the other countries.

Nevertheless, a contracting country may refuse or cancel the registrations of the following marks:

1. Marks which are of such a nature as to infringe rights acquired by third parties in the country in question.

2. Marks which have no distinctive character, or which consist exclusively of signs or indications which serve in trade to designate the kind, quality, quantity, destination, value, place of origin of the goods, or date of production or which have become customary in the current language, or in the bona fide and recognized customs of the trade of the country in question.

In arriving at a decision as to the distinctive character of a mark, all the circumstances of the case must be taken into account, including the length of time during which the mark has been in use.

3. Marks which are contrary to morality or public order.

It is understood that a mark cannot be considered as contrary to public order for the sole reason that it does not conform to some stipulation of the laws concerning marks, except when such stipulation itself relates to public order.

ARTICLE 4.

Any person who has duly filed an application for the registration of a trade mark in one of the contracting countries, or his legal representative or assignee, shall enjoy, for the purposes of filing in the other countries, a right of priority during twelve months.

Consequently, a subsequent filing in any of the other countries before the expiration of this period shall not be refused or invalidated by reason of any acts accomplished in the interval, for instance, by another filing, by use of the mark, etc.

The above period starts from the date of filing of the first application in one of the contracting countries and terminates on the anniversary of the same date. If the last day of the period is a holiday in the country where protection is claimed, the period shall be extended until the first following working day.

ARTICLE 5.

The contracting countries undertake to refuse or to cancel, either administratively if their legislation so permits, or at the request of an interested party, the registration of any trade mark which is a reproduction of or an imitation capable of creating confusion with a mark known in the country of registration as being already the mark of a person entitled to the benefits of this convention and utilized for the same or similar classes of goods.

The fact of the mark's being so known in the country in question may be proved by the interested party by any means of evidence.

A period of at least three years shall be allowed for claiming the removal of such marks. This period shall run from the date of registration of the mark.

There shall be no limit to the period within which application may be made for the removal of marks when it is proved that the registrant had knowledge of the ownership, employment or use of the mark in any of the contracting countries by a person entitled to the benefits of this convention.

ARTICLE 6.

Any registrations effected in one of the contracting countries by an agent, representative or customer of the owner of a trade mark previously used in one of the other countries shall, in the absence of other proof, be regarded as belonging to the said prior owner of the trade mark and inure to his benefit.

ARTICLE 7.

The use of a trade mark by its proprietor in a form different on minor or non-substantial elements from the form in which it has been registered in any of the contracting countries shall not entail forfeiture of the registration or protection of the mark. Similarly the non-use of the mark for certain of the goods of the list which was declared at the time of registration shall not affect the protection of the mark.

In case the form of the mark is substantially changed, or the list of goods, in connection with which it is used, is modified or enlarged, the proprietor of the mark may be required to apply for a new registration, without prejudice to the protection of the original mark or of the use in connection with the original list of goods.

ARTICLE 8.

Trade names of persons entitled to the benefits of this convention shall be protected in all the contracting countries. Such protection shall be enjoyed without necessity of deposit or registration, whether or not the trade name forms part of a trade mark.

ARTICLE 9.

All goods bearing illegally a trade mark or trade name shall be seized on importation into those contracting countries where the mark or name has a right to legal protection.

Seizure shall be effected equally in the country where the mark or name was illegally applied, or in the country into which the goods bearing it may have been imported.

The seizure shall take place at the request either of the public prosecutor or of any other competent authority or of any interested party whether an individual or a body of persons corporate or incorporate in conformity with the domestic law of each country.

The authorities shall not be bound to effect the seizure of goods in transit.

If the laws of a country do not admit of seizure on importation, such seizure shall be replaced by prohibition of importation or seizure within the country.

If the laws of any country do not admit either of seizure upon importation, or of prohibition of importation, or of seizure within the country, and pending the requisite modification of these laws, these measures shall be replaced by the remedies available in such cases to nationals.

ARTICLE 10.

The contracting countries undertake to protect indications of place of origin of products.

The stipulations of the preceding article shall be applicable to all goods which bear a false indication of origin calculated to deceive the public in the country in which its repression is sought.

Any producer, manufacturer or trader, whether an individual or a body of persons corporate or incorporate, engaged in the production, manufacture, or trade of such goods, and established either in the locality falsely indicated as the place of origin, in the district where the locality is situated, or in the country falsely indicated shall in in any case be deemed a party interested.

In the absence of any special remedies ensuring the repression of false indications of origin, the remedies provided by the corresponding stipulations of the laws relating to trade marks or trade names shall be applicable.

ARTICLE 11.

The contracting countries are bound to assure to persons entitled to the benefits of the present convention an effective protection against unfair competition.

Every act of competition contrary to honest practices in industrial or commercial matters constitutes an act of unfair competition.

The following acts among others shall be prohibited:

1. All acts of such a nature as to create confusion by any means whatsoever with the goods of a competitor.

2. All acts of such a nature as to injure wrongfully the business relations of a manufacturer or merchant by any means whatsoever.

In the absence of any special remedies ensuring the repression of acts of unfair competition and pending the requisite enactment of a law of unfair competition, the remedies provided by the corresponding stipulations of the laws relating to trade marks or trade names shall be applicable.

ARTICLE 12.

The present convention shall be ratified and the ratifications shall be deposited at Washington not later than the 1st of June, 1930. It shall come into force, between the countries which shall have ratified it, one month after that date. From that moment it shall supersede any previous conventions relating to trade marks, trade names and indications of place of origin between the contracting countries.

ARTICLE 13.

The signatory countries which will not ratify this convention in due time may accede to it later. The accession shall be notified to the Pan American Union and by the latter to all the contracting countries. It shall entail as a matter of right accession to all the clauses, and admission to all the advantages stipulated in the present convention and shall take effect one month after the dispatch of the notification by the Pan American Union to the contracting countries.

Any contracting country may denounce the convention by notifying the Pan American Union. The latter shall communicate such notice to the contracting countries. The denunciation shall take effect one year from the date of the receipt of notice thereof by the Pan American Union, without prejudice, however, to rights acquired under the convention.

COMMENTS ON THE PROPOSED DRAFT

1. Scope of the Convention

Article 1.

The first article of the Convention should display its scope. In the Convention of 1910 the first article declared that the contracting States enter into the convention for the protection of trade marks and trade names; article VIII provided for the protection of indications of origin; and article XI proclaimed that a Union of American Nations was constituted for the purposes of the convention. The Convention of 1923 omitted entirely the provisions of the first article of the Convention of 1910. In the International Convention of 1883–1925 there is a provision displaying the scope of the convention in article I.

The Convention of 1910, in articles IV and V, contained a definition of trade marks and excluded certain things from being used as such. These provisions were discarded in the Convention of 1923. No attempt is made here to adopt similar provisions. But the question of conception of trade marks is affected by the proposed article 3, and that of trade names by article 8. A definition of unfair competition is included in article 11.

2. Persons Protected by the Convention and National Treatment Principle

Article 2.

This article follows the wording of article 2 of the International Convention of 1883–1925, with one exception referring to the persons protected. That Convention entitles to its benefits three classes of persons: nationals of each of the contracting countries, nationals of non-contracting countries domiciled in the Union, and nationals of non-contracting countries possessing industrial or commercial establishments in the Union. The Pan American

Convention of 1910 took no account of the nationality, domicile or establishment of a person. It was sufficient that a mark had been registered in any of the contracting countries. The Convention of 1923 entitled to its benefits only persons domiciled in any of the contracting countries. This would seem to conform to a common principle of public law in Latin American countries.

For the purposes of protection of trade marks, trade names, etc., it would seem that the provision of the proposed article is most adequate. That which is sought to protect is the foreign trade and business relations of persons carrying on business in the contracting countries. Nationals, therefore, of such countries carrying on business in non-contracting countries, for instance, in Great Britain or France, may properly be excluded from the benefits of the convention. On the other hand domicile alone is not a sufficient basis. The owner of a trade mark may be domiciled in a non-contracting country, but his business establishment may be located in one of the contracting countries and form part of the industry and trade of such country. Moreover, the word domicile raises difficulties of interpretation, while the possession of a business establishment is a factual situation.

The article stipulates the national treatment principle of the International Convention of 1883–1925. It is a principle which figured in all the earlier Pan American Conventions on industrial property, but which, curiously enough, is not contained in the Conventions of 1910 and 1923. Under this principle all discriminations between nationals and "unionist" persons in any of the contracting countries are abolished. Also the strict rule of reciprocity is done away with. Each of the contracting countries must admit the persons entitled to the benefits of the convention to all advantages, rights, protection, and remedies available to nationals. It is a salutary principle, which has been applied for over forty years in the Industrial Property Union. It guarantees the security and certainty of the rights. The formalities, conditions, and obligations imposed by the municipal law of each country are applicable to nationals as well as to the "unionist" persons, so far as they are not derogated from by the other provisions of the convention.

Article 2 of the International Convention of 1883–1925 contains two more paragraphs. They are not taken in the proposed article as being only of an interpretative character.

3. Admission of Trade Marks to Registration

Article 3.

This article, with two changes, is taken from article 6 of the International Convention of 1883–1925. It purports to secure the validation of trade marks throughout the Union. It establishes the rule that a trade mark acquired in one of the contracting countries must be recognized and protected in the other countries in its original form. A number of well-defined exceptions in which this rule may not be applied are enumerated. For no other reasons but those indicated may a trade mark be refused registration and protection on the ground that its form is not in accordance with the trade mark law of the country where registration and protection is claimed.

The rule is explained by the nature of trade marks. The law of the different countries differs as to what may be a lawful trade mark. If foreigners should be strictly assimilated to nationals, their trade marks would be protected only if they fulfill the requirements of the law of each country. This would mean that a trade mark valid under the law of the country of origin of the proprietor, but invalid under the law of a foreign country into which his products are imported, would not be protected in the latter country. A way out for the manufacturer or trader would be to change his mark in order to satisfy the law of each country. This would amount to a denial of protection. The whole purpose and function of trade marks would be defeated; the reputation attached to the original trade mark would be destroyed to a large degree.

It is thus highly important for the adequate protection of trade marks that they should be validated in all the countries in their original form. But this should necessarily be subject to certain limitations imposed by a due consideration of the rights of third parties, whether the latter are owners of the same mark in the other countries or the general public which uses freely the subject-matter of the trade mark as a descriptive, generic or geographical designation. Besides, the public order of a country may be opposed to the protection of a trade mark, by reason of its being against the good morals or public policy. These limitations are taken care of in the three exceptions enumerated in the article.

The differences of the proposed article from article 6 of the International Convention of 1883–1925 are the following:

The latter limits the application of the above rule of validation only to trade marks duly registered in the country of origin. The proposed article includes in the rule all trade marks legally protected in any of the contracting countries. The difference concerns: (*a*) the country in which the mark is originated; and (*b*) the condition of the trade mark in such country.

It is suggested to do away with the conception of country of origin, as the American, British, German, and many other delegations proposed at the Conference of The Hague of the Industrial Property Union.[1] A manufacturer or

[1] *Actes de la Conférence de La Haye*, pp. 340, 442, 444.

trader may use several trade marks in connection with his foreign trade which he does not use in his own country. In the modern conditions of business, the provisions of article 6 of the International Convention adopted as far back as 1883 seem obsolete.

Nor is it reasonable to limit the application of the rule of validation to registered marks. If a mark is legally protected in one of the contracting countries, whether ownership therein is acquired by adoption and use or by registration, it should be validated in its original form. Many trade marks in the United States are acquired by adoption and use. No valid reason exists why they should not be admitted to registration and protection in the other countries.

The proposed difference from article 6 of the International Convention conforms with the scope of article II of the draft prepared by the Pan American Union, which, consequently, becomes unnecessary.

4. Protection of Priority of Trade Marks

Articles 4 and 5.

The first of these articles follows the wording of article 4 of the International Convention of 1883–1925, with one or two differences. It stipulates for a right of priority for a person who deposits first a trade mark in any of the contracting countries. The scope and utility of this stipulation is explained above.[1] A similar right of priority was granted by the Pan American Convention of 1910, article III. The Convention of 1923 contained no such stipulation, its article II proclaiming a totally different rule, which is discussed above.[2]

The period of the right of priority for trade marks is fixed to six months by article 4 of the International Con-

[1] See *supra*, p. 42.
[2] See *supra*, p. 26.

vention of 1883–1925. In view of the great distances separating the various American countries and their special trade conditions, the proposal here is to extend this period to twelve months. Following this proposal, the third paragraph contains the rules of computation of the period. All of them are taken from the International Convention of 1883–1925, with the exception of the provision that the period terminates on the anniversary of the same date. This aims at securing a uniform computation of the period in all the contracting countries, which is not fully accomplished in the Industrial Property Union.

The second of the above articles is also taken from the International Convention of 1883–1925, where it figures as article 6bis, and was adopted at the last Conference of revision, at The Hague. The purpose of that article is explained above.[1] Its effect is that the registrant's right in a mark registered in any of the contracting countries is not conclusive before the lapse of a three year period from such registration or without limit of time in case the registration was made in bad faith. In other words, in the member countries of the Industrial Property Union where property in a trade mark is acquired by priority of registration (for instance, in Germany, Japan, Norway, Poland, etc.) a limitation is introduced in favor of persons entitled to the benefits of the Convention. Such persons may challenge the right of the registrant, show a better right, and, eventually, obtain the cancellation of the registration. The better right which may be shown and cause the cancellation of the registration is a prior use of the trade mark by the applicant in the country where such cancellation is sought. However, not any prior use is sufficient for this purpose, but a use of the mark to such an extent that the competent authority will decide that the mark was, at the time of

[1] See *supra*, p. 43.

registration, well-known in the country as belonging to the applicant and utilized by him for the same or similar classes of goods.

A stipulation which tends to protect vested trade mark rights and which was adopted by the thirty-eight countries of the Industrial Property Union may and must assuredly be adopted by the twenty-one countries of the Pan American Union. Such a stipulation would go a long way towards solving one of the most important problems of the Inter-American régime of trade marks.

The question is whether anything more may be desired in the relations between the American countries. The article proposed here presents certain differences from article 6bis of the International Convention of 1883–1925, calculated to adapt the latter to the conditions of the American countries. It should be recalled that article 6bis of the International Convention has been adopted in 1925 and has not yet come into effect as between all the member countries of the Industrial Property Union, so that no experience of its practical working is yet available. It should be possible to improve upon it, therefore, in view of the experience with similar provisions of the Pan American Conventions.

The first change proposed concerns the extent of the prior use in one of the contracting countries of a trade mark owned by a manufacturer or trader domiciled or established in another. Article 6bis of the International Convention, which extends its protection to a mark "*considered by the competent authority of the country of registration to be well-known in the country as being already the mark of a person . . . ,*" is fitted to the industrial and commercial conditions of the European countries especially. In most of the American countries this provision is too indefinite and vague in view of the lack of an adequate degree of industrial and commercial organization which may keep track and be aware of any new trade mark appearing on foreign products. The business relations established in each country by manufacturers or traders carrying on business in other countries are often isolated, disconnected, and individualized. Thus, a trade mark may be used for a long time in connection with such business relations, yet be considered as not "well-known in the country" as being the mark of a certain person. It is proposed, therefore, to make the provision in question less strict. This would be accomplished by the proposed expression *"a mark known in the country of registration,"* and by the additional second paragraph which provides that such knowledge of the mark may be proved by any means of evidence.

A second change from article 6bis of the International Convention concerns marks registered in bad faith. It is not clear in the provision of that article whether bad faith may exist when the registrant had knowledge of the mark's being used by another in a foreign country or only in the country of registration. The proposed last paragraph of article V makes this clear. Bad faith clearly exists when the registrant obtained the registration of the mark with knowledge of its being adopted, used or owned by another. It is immaterial where such adoption or use takes place.

It is believed that the proposed article constitutes a sound solution of the problem of protection of the priority of trade marks — a solution which should be satisfactory to all the American countries for the reasons explained above. It brings the necessary attenuations to the stipulations on priority of trade marks of the Pan American Conventions of 1910 and 1923, which will make the new Convention acceptable to all parties. The draft prepared by the Pan American Union, articles VII and XII, proposes a solution of the priority problem which will not be acceptable to many a Latin American country. It transfers the provisions of the Convention of 1923 and adds thereto the stipulations of article 6bis of the International Convention.

5. Protection of Ownership of Trade Marks

Article 6.

This article is taken from the draft prepared by the Pan American Union. It contains a stipulation which should be accepted by all the contracting countries. It tends to defeat fraudulent attempts of persons having dealings with a trade mark owner from misappropriating his mark, and thus profiting of the patronage connected with the mark. In this respect, their registration comes under the provision of the last paragraph of the preceding article. The effect, however, of this stipulation is that no prior use in the country or proof of the fraud of the registrant is necessary. The applicant need only show that the registrant was his agent, representative or customer. On such proof the registrant's name must be taken off the register and the true owner's name must be substituted instead. This is provided for by the law of many countries and is justified by the close relation between the owner and his agent. The latter may only maintain his registration by proving a transfer of the mark to him by the owner.

6. Use of the Mark in a Different Form or with Different Goods

Article 7.

This article is inspired by certain provisions of articles 7 and 9 of the Madrid Trade Mark Arrangement of 1891–1925. In these provisions no distinction is made between minor and substantial changes in the form of the mark, although the above distinction between reduction and extension or modification of the list of goods, on which the mark is to be applied, is adopted. The first paragraph does not so much tend to permit changes in the form of the mark as to eliminate the danger of forfeiting its protection or having the registration cancelled by reason alone of a slight omission or addition of a sign or word in the trade mark. In certain American countries on this account trade mark owners incur a serious danger of losing their rights in their marks. What the above stipulation tends to do is to allow such slight changes which in no way affect the distinctive character of a trade mark.[1]

7. Protection of Trade Names

Article 8.

The proposed stipulation is taken from article 8 of the International Convention of 1883–1925 and from the Pan American Conventions of 1910 and 1923. Curiously enough, the draft prepared by the Pan American Union contains no provision for the protection of trade names. The differences of the proposed article from the stipulations of the previous Conventions are: (*a*) that it is separated into two distinct periods. The first is set apart to make it certain that there is a clear obligation of each of the contracting countries to protect trade names; (*b*) The term "*nom commercial*" of the International Convention of 1883–1925 and "*nombres comerciales*" of the Spanish text of the Pan American Conventions is rendered by the term "trade name" and not "commercial name." Such a rendering is more accurate as the term "*nom commercial*" is as broad as the term "trade name," applying not only to names of persons or firms but also of business establishments and of goods.

[1] In this respect article 105 of the Brazilian Decree No. 16,264 of December 19, 1923 provides: "The registered marks should not undergo any alteration, either in the illustrative signs, nor in the phrases, numbers or words, which distinguish them." If the phrase "which distinguish them" refers to the substantial and distinctive elements of a mark, the Brazilian law establishes the rule which is embodied in the proposed article.

8. Special Remedies Against Infringements

Article 9.

This article follows the wording of article 9 of the International Convention of 1883–1925. Its purpose and effect in the Industrial Property Union is explained above.[1] Since no immediate obligation is imposed on the contracting countries to create domestic law in accordance with this article, there should be no difficulty for all such countries to adopt this article.

Article X of the draft prepared by the Pan American Union would not seem to be altogether consistent with this article. For the rest, it duplicates the provisions of article 2 and is, therefore, unnecessary.

9. Protection of Indications of Place of Origin

Article 10.

This article aims at protecting indications of place of origin of products. Its first paragraph contains an explicit engagement of the contracting countries in this respect. It is well-known, however, that many original appellations indicating the origin or place of production of goods have become generic, descriptive or geographical terms in the current language of commerce. It is important, therefore, to determine the cases in which statements as to the place of origin are to be protected.

In the Industrial Property Union no agreement could be obtained on this point, and a dual regulation has resulted. All the member countries agreed on a stipulation in article 10 of the International Convention tending to repress what is termed a "qualified fraud" with respect to indications of origin. False indications of origin are to be repressed when they are used together with a fictitious trade name or one borrowed with fraudulent intention. A number of the

[1] See *supra*, p. 45.

member countries of the Union, however, entered into the Madrid Arrangement of 1891 under which the repression of false indications of origin is unqualified.

It is submitted that the propositions of the Cuban, American and other delegations at the Conference of The Hague of the Industrial Property Union would seem to satisfy most adequately the needs of Inter-American trade.[1] They are embodied in the second paragraph of the proposed article.

The third paragraph is taken from the International Convention of 1883-1925 (article 10, par. 2). The fourth paragraph is taken from the Madrid Arrangement of 1891–1925 for the repression of false indications of origin (article 1, last paragraph), and tends to afford an immediate sanction to the stipulations of the article, in case the law of a country contains no provisions for the protection of indications of place of origin.

It is to be noted that the Pan American Conventions of 1910 and 1923 contained certain provisions purporting to protect indications of origin, but these provisions were vague and indefinite. (See articles VIII of the Convention of 1910 and article V, sections 1 and 5 of the Convention of 1923). The draft prepared by the Pan American Union contains no provisions for the protection of indications of place of origin.

10. Repression of Unfair Competition

Article 11.

This article follows the wording of article 10bis of the International Convention of 1883–1925, with the exception of the second part of the third paragraph and the fourth paragraph. The purpose and effect of article 10bis in the

[1] *Actes de la Conférence de La Haye*, p. 472.

Industrial Property Union is indicated above.[1] The second class of acts of unfair competition prohibited in that article consists of false allegations, in the course of trade, of such a nature as to discredit the goods of a competitor. In this form, the provision covers a part only of the acts which may injure the good will and business relations of a person although no confusion with his goods is produced. For this reason the proposed article makes this class of acts more general and broad, so as to cover such acts as enticing of employees, intimidation of customers, etc.

As in the case of indications of place of origin, the last paragraph purports to afford an immediate sanction to the provisions of this article. Thus, unless and until the law of unfair competition in each of the contracting countries affords adequate remedies against acts of unfair competition, such acts shall be repressed as acts of infringement of trade marks or trade names are repressed under the existing law. In other words, in the above case, an act of unfair competition shall be treated as an act of infringement.

The draft prepared by the Pan American Union proposes a stipulation (article XVII) similar to that of the International Convention of 1883–1925. It is submitted that the stipulation proposed here should be preferred for the above reasons. The last paragraph of article XVII of the draft of the Pan American Union, taken from the Convention of 1923, does not seem to be connected with the whole article. Besides, its effect is covered by article X proposed here.

11. Coming Into Effect of the New Convention, Accessions and Denunciations

Articles 12 and 13.

The substance of these articles is taken from the corresponding provisions of the International Convention of

[1] See *supra*, p. 50.

1883–1925, from previous Pan American Conventions, and from the draft prepared by the Pan American Union.

B. Arrangement for the Inter-American Registration of Trade Marks.

One is very sceptical on the advisability of preparing and adopting an arrangement for the Inter-American registration of trade marks when one has in mind the very small number of trade marks registered at the Havana Bureau during the 1919–1927 period. Yet, similar is the history of the first years of registration at the Berne Bureau of the Industrial Property Union, under the Madrid Trade Mark Arrangement.[1] The institution of an Inter-American Bureau for registration of trade marks in the American countries may appeal and be beneficial to small business men having a limited export trade and desirous of saving the fees and expenses necessitated by registration in each of the American countries through trade mark agents and solicitors. Besides, this Bureau might fulfill the same function as the Bureau of the Industrial Property Union with respect to collecting and distributing data on the legislation, administrative practice, and court decisions of the various countries. It is well-known that it is very difficult to interested persons to get at original sources in this regard.

The international registration at the Bureau of the Industrial Property Union at Berne is based on a different principle than the Inter-American registration under the Conventions of 1910 and 1923. Under the Madrid Trade Mark Arrangement the Bureau at Berne registers the marks transmitted to it by the administration of one of the contracting coun-

[1] From 1893 to 1900 the marks registered at the Bureau numbered 2391 and originated from six only out of the eleven countries, parties to the Arrangement. See *General Statement of the Service of International Registration of Trade Marks 1893–1924*, Berne, 1926, p. 25.

tries and notifies the other countries of such registration. Unless these countries declare within a year their refusal to protect a mark registered by the Bureau, registration at the Bureau is tantamount to registration in each of the contracting countries. The effects of such registration last uniformly for twenty years in all the contracting countries in which protection was not refused. The applicant pays only an international registration fee of 150 Swiss francs and of 75 for each additional mark filed at the same time. A part of these fees serves to defray the expenses of the international registration and the balance is distributed equally between the contracting countries.

Under the Conventions of 1910 and 1923 the trade marks transmitted by the administrations of the American countries to the Inter-American Bureau are not registered by the latter. They are transmitted to the contracting countries for registration. The fees and charges payable to the Bureau, under the Convention of 1923, include a fee for the expenses of the Bureau and the registration fees payable on direct registration in each of countries where the mark is transmitted for registration. No uniform duration of the effects of registration was provided for. No limitations of the reasons for which registration might be refused by one of the contracting countries was indicated. And no period was fixed within which the refusal should be notified to the Bureau.

It is not believed that the principle of the Madrid Trade Mark Arrangement for a central registration by the Bureau may be accepted by the American countries. But the other provisions of that Arrangement which purport to ensure speedy registration, eliminate arbitrary refusals, and accomplish a uniform duration of protection, might be adopted in the Inter-American Arrangement.

The draft convention prepared by the Pan American

Union purports to transfer into the regime of Inter-American registration some of the above provisions of the Madrid Trade Mark Arrangement. To that extent, the draft raises no objections. A number of its stipulations are to be amended with a view of making them consistent with the general convention which is discussed above. Of course, the articles of the draft of the Pan American Union which refer to general questions of trade mark protection and unfair competition are to be omitted, as being taken care of by the proposed general convention.

Under these conditions, the following draft is submitted. It is accompanied by notes whenever a comment is necessary.

ARTICLE 1

Persons domiciled or who have real and effective industrial or commercial establishments in any of the contracting countries may secure in all the others the protection of their trade marks registered or deposited in any of them by transmitting such marks to the Inter-American Bureau established at . . .

Note. Article I of the draft prepared by the Pan American Union is put in this form by reason of the character of this Arrangement. This form follows the wording of article I of the Madrid Trade Mark Arrangement. Moreover, it is made to conform to the above proposed general convention.

ARTICLE 2

The proprietor of a mark registered or deposited in any of the contracting countries shall, through the Trade Mark Office of such country, file with the Inter-American Bureau an application in accordance with the provisions of the Appendix to this Arrangement, which is declared to be a part hereof, and at the same time a fee equivalent to two hundred and fifty dollars ($250.00) United States gold.

Note. This article is based on article IV of the draft of the Pan American Union.

ARTICLE 3

Immediately upon receipt of the application provided in the preceding article the Inter-American Bureau shall transmit by registered mail copies of the same, accompanied by the payments as provided in article 10 to the

Trade Mark Offices of those countries which shall have ratified or adhered to this Arrangement, except the country of origin, retaining the copies and payments intended for countries which have not yet ratified this Arrangement until such time as they do so, if within three years of the coming into effect of the Arrangement, transmitting accumulated copies of the applications and accumulated fees to them after such ratification in accordance with that article.

Note. This article is taken from the draft of the Pan American Union (article V).

ARTICLE 4

Each contracting country, through the responsible official of its Trade Mark Office, shall promptly acknowledge the receipt of each application, transmitted by the Inter-American Bureau, and in due course shall report what action has been taken thereon; but, unless within six months from the date of such receipt, notice to the contrary is received by the Inter-American Bureau, it shall be presumed that the mark is admitted to deposit or registration in the contracting countries.

A contracting country may declare its refusal to admit to registration and protection a mark transmitted by the Inter-American Bureau only in the cases provided for in article 3 of the Convention for the Protection of Trade Marks, Trade Names and Indications of Origin and for the Repression of Unfair Competition signed at Washington, ..., 1929.

Any declaration of refusal received by the Inter-American Bureau shall be transmitted to the Trade Mark Office of the country of origin, the proprietor of the mark, and his agents if such are indicated in the application, provided for in article 2.

The interested party shall have the same rights against such refusal of protection as if the mark was directly filed in the country where registration is refused. The declaration of refusal shall specify the grounds of refusal and indicate the legal provisions on which such refusal is based and the period within which an appeal against such refusal may be taken. Such period shall begin 120 days after the date on which notice of the refusal has been sent to the Inter-American Bureau.

Note. With the exception of the first paragraph which is based on article VI the draft of the Pan American Bureau and the last part of the last paragraph which is based on article VIII of the same draft, the rest of the proposed article is taken from the Madrid Trade Mark Arrangement as revised at The Hague in 1925 (article 5).

ARTICLE 5

A trade mark filed with the Inter-American Bureau and transmitted by it for registration to the contracting countries shall enjoy the right of priority provided for in article 4 of the Convention for the Protection of Trade Marks, Trade Names and Indications of Origin and for the Repression of Unfair Competition, signed at Washington, ..., 1929.

Note. This article is based on article 4, par. 2 of the Madrid Trade Mark Arrangement of 1891–1925.

ARTICLE 6

Subject to the condition that protection must continue to be enjoyed in the country in which the proprietor is domiciled or possesses real and effective industrial or commercial establishments, the period of protection of a trade mark registered through the Inter-American Bureau shall be fifteen years calculated from the date of filing the application at the Inter-American Bureau, and shall be renewed for successive periods of fifteen years, each by filing an application for renewal in advance of the date of expiration of the period of protection.

Note. This article is based on article III of the draft of the Pan American Union. Some slight modifications in form are made.

ARTICLE 7

A valid transfer of the ownership of a mark in the country of first registration or deposit shall have the same force in the other contracting countries that it would have if the transfer had taken place originally within their respective jurisdictions and in accordance with their respective laws, provided that the notice of transfer given to the Inter-American Bureau shall be accompanied by a fee equivalent to fifty dollars ($50.00) United States gold. Of this sum ten dollars ($10.00) shall be retained by the Inter-American Bureau and two dollars ($2.00) remitted with the notice of transfer of the ownership of the mark, to each of the countries party to the convention, other than the country of origin of the mark.

In each signatory country the ownership of a mark may be transferred for that country independently of ownership in any other country in accordance with the provisions of the law relating to the transfer of marks registered under the laws of such country.

Note. Taken from article IX of the draft of the Pan American Union

ARTICLE 8

In order to give effect to the purpose of this Arrangement, the High Contracting Parties establish as sole international agency the Inter-American Bureau in ....; and they confer upon the official correspondence of that Bureau the postal frank.

Note. Taken from article XIV of the draft of the Pan American Union.

ARTICLE 9

The Inter-American Bureau shall have the duties enumerated in the Appendix to this Arrangement, and shall be maintained after January 1, 1935, wholly by its proportion of the fees received under this Arrangement provided in article 10; but until that date the Bureau shall be maintained in part by contributions from the governments of the contracting countries in accordance with the population of each as follows:

Population	*Contribution*
50,000,000 or more	$10,000
25,000,000 to 50,000,000	5,000
10,000,000 to 25,000,000	3,000
5,000,000 to 10,000,000	2,000
Less than 5,000,000	1,000

Note. Taken from article XV of the draft of the Pan American Union.

ARTICLE 10

Of each payment of two hundred and fifty dollars ($250.00) made at the time of the application for protection under the provisions of this convention, the sum of fifty dollars ($50.00) shall be retained by the Inter-American Bureau, and the balance shall be distributed in equal payments of ten dollars ($10.00) among all the contracting countries, other than the country of origin of the mark, as soon as they shall have ratified or adhered to this Arrangement.

Three years after the coming into effect of this Arrangement the money held on deposit by the Bureau and intended to be paid to the countries which may not have ratified or adhered to this Arrangement, either for the registration of a mark as set forth in this article or for the transfer of a mark as set forth in article 7, shall be remitted through the respective Trade Mark Offices to the proprietors of the marks theretofore applying to the Bureau for the registration or transfer of such marks.

Three years after the coming into effect of this Arrange-

ment the amount to be remitted to the Inter-American Bureau by the proprietor of a mark through the Trade Mark Office of the country of his domicile, for the registration of a mark as set forth in article 2 or for the transfer of a mark as set forth in article 7 of this Arrangement, shall be reduced by ten dollars ($10.00) and two dollars ($2.00) respectively, United States gold, for each country that may not be a party to this Arrangement at the time application is made for the registration or transfer of a mark.

Note. Taken from article XVI of the draft of the Pan American Union.

ARTICLE 11

This Arrangement shall be ratified and the ratifications shall be deposited at Washington not later than the 1st of June, 1930. It shall come into force, between the countries which shall have ratified it, one month after that date. From that moment it shall supersede any previous conventions relating to the Inter-American registration of trade marks.

ARTICLE 12

The signatory countries of the Convention for the Protection of Trade Marks, Trade Names, and Indications of Place of Origin and for the Repression of Unfair Competition, signed at Washington, ..., 1929, which will not ratify this convention may accede to it later. The accession shall be notified to the Pan American Union and by the latter to all the contracting countries. It shall entail as a matter of right accession to all the clauses, and admission to all the advantages stipulated in the present Arrangement and shall take effect one month after the dispatch of the notification by the Pan American Union to the contracting countries.

Any country may denounce this Arrangement by notifying the Pan American Union. The latter shall communicate such notice to the contracting countries. The denunciation shall take effect one year from the date of the receipt of notice thereof by the Pan American Union without prejudice, however, to rights acquired under the Arrangement.

Note. These two articles are identical with those of the general convention and are taken substantially from corresponding provisions of the International Convention of 1883–1925, the previous Pan American Conventions, and the draft of the Pan American Union.

The Pan American Union has also prepared a draft of Regulations to be appended to this Arrangement. It is submitted that such draft be adopted with a few modifications in form.

C. Resolution Recommending a Model-Law of Unfair Competition

In a previous part of this study[1] it is described how in many countries in recent years special legislation was enacted with a view of repressing acts of unfair competition. This was resorted to, especially, when the legal materials at hand did not afford sufficient elasticity as to satisfy the growing needs for protection of business relations. The same case seems to be presented in Latin American countries. The enactment of a special law of unfair competition in each of these countries would be a wise measure of social engineering for the protection of their social order from acts of deceit and fraud against competitors and the buying public.

In the United States of America the law of unfair competition is a case law constituted by a body of decisions, and is of a comparatively recent birth and development. It rested for some time on the basic principle that no man has the right to pass off his goods upon the public for the goods of another. On this principle all acts causing confusion between the business activities of two persons were repressed. The most recent cases seem to surpass that principle, making as the basis of the law the protection of business relations regardless of a confusion between the goods of two producers.[2]

Mr. Ed. S. Rogers, an authority on unfair competition law in the United States, has prepared a "Uniform Code

[1] See *supra*, pp. 57 ff.

[2] Vogue Co. *v.* Thompson-Hudson Co. (1924) 300 Fed. 509. Yale Electric Corporation *v.* Robertson (1928) 26 F. (2d) 972.

dealing with Unfair Competition," which he has kindly communicated to the present writer. This draft extracts the United States law on unfair competition from the existing body of court decisions of the United States. Thus the draft contains rules of law embodying the judicial experience of a great commercial and industrial country and not simply an aggregate of rules obtained by theoretical reasoning and logical deduction. The only defect of the draft is that it is too indefinite for Latin American countries which have not the background of common law and for which, therefore, the terms of the draft have no definite legal meaning and significance.

The present writer has attempted to adapt Mr. Rogers's draft to the special acts on unfair competition of the various European countries.[1] As Latin American countries are governed by the general civil law, the terms and legal phraseology of the acts on unfair competition of European countries possess a more definite meaning in Latin America.

The Pan American Trade Mark Conference should consider and discuss this draft of a model-law of unfair competition. It is submitted that a resolution be adopted recommending to the various American countries the enactment of such a law. A draft of such a resolution and of the model-law on unfair competition are printed here.

RESOLUTION

The Conference of representatives of the American countries convened at Washington, D. C., on February 11, 1929, for the purpose of studying in its amplest scope the problem of the Inter-American protection of trade marks;

Whereas the above problem cannot be satisfactorily and adequately solved unless special legislation for the repression of acts of unfair competition be enacted in each of the contracting countries where no well-establ-ished law of unfair competition exists;

[1] The Acts used in this respect are enumerated above, pp. 48–49.

Whereas a model-law of unfair competition was considered, discussed and adopted by this Conference and is appended hereto;

Whereas the model-law in question represents the law of unfair competition of many countries of the world and conforms to the most recent enactments of such countries;

Recommends

To the American countries the enactment of a special law on unfair competition adopting the principles and rules of the model-law appended to this resolution.

Model Law Against Unfair Competition

§ 1. Every act of competition contrary to honest practices in industrial or commercial matters constitutes an act of unfair competition. All such acts are declared unlawful and are forbidden.

By way of enumeration but not of limitation unfair competition shall include the acts indicated in the following articles.

Note. This general principle is taken from article 1 of the Law of Unfair Competition of Germany, Austria, Hungary, Greece, Latvia, and Czechoslovakia, and also from Article 10bis of the International Convention of 1883–1925.

The second sentence of the first paragraph and the second paragraph are taken from Mr. Rogers's draft.

§ 2. All acts whatsoever calculated to represent that the goods or business of one manufacturer or trader are the goods or business of another, are prohibited whether such representation be made directly or indirectly by the appropriation, confusing use, or simulation of trade marks, trade names or other distinguishing names or symbols, the imitation of labels, containers, wrappings, get-up of goods, invoices, advertisements, catalogues or other means of identification.

§ 3. All acts whatsoever of a nature to injure wrongfully the business relations of a manufacturer or trader are prohibited. Such acts are declared to be especially:

(a) Allegations of facts on the goods, the person or the business of a manufacturer or trader of a nature to injure the carrying on the business of the latter or the credit of the owner of the business;

(b) Acts accomplished with the intention of inducing a breach of contract with a manufacturer or trader;

(c) Acts of commercial bribery;

(d) Acts of interference with contracts with employees

of a manufacturer or trader, such as offering pecuniary advantages to employees of an enterprise to incite them to grant illegitimate favors or enticing employees to obtain confidential information;

(e) Acts of intimidation or oppression of competitors' customers;

(f) Violation or misuse of business or trade secrets.

Note. These two sections are based on Mr. Rogers's draft, but are modified and adapted to the Unfair Competition Acts of the above countries.

§ 4. Any use of false indications of geographical origin, and of false descriptions of goods is prohibited.

Note. Taken from Mr. Rogers's draft.

§ 5. Whoever commits or abets acts of unfair competition shall be liable to an action for damages and also to a decree against the continuance thereof by any person injured thereby.

A suit for an injunction against acts of unfair competition may also be brought by professional or business associations constituted for the protection of industrial or commercial interests.

Note. This section is taken from Mr. Rogers's draft but is adapted to the German and Austrian Acts.

§ 6. Whenever acts of unfair competition are accomplished with fraudulent intention, the persons liable therefor shall be subject to the penalties provided for by the Law on Trade Marks for the cases of fraudulent infringement of trade marks.

Note. This section is taken from the German and Austrian Acts.

§ 7. It is forbidden to import, export, manufacture, distribute, sell or offer for sale goods in connection with which an act of unfair competition has been committed, as provided in the preceding articles.

The importation of such goods shall be prohibited at the initiative of the customs administration or at the request of any interested party.

§ 8. Goods in connection with which an act of unfair competition is committed may be seized at the request of the interested party. In case a violation of this law is proved, the seized goods shall be forfeited or destroyed or the unlawful marking thereon removed or obliterated at the discretion of the Tribunal, which shall take into account all the circumstances of the case.

Note. The two last sections are based on Rogers's draft, but follow the wording of Acts of the civil law countries.

APPENDICES

APPENDICES

I.

Convention for the Protection of Trade Marks Signed at Buenos Aires, August 20, 1910.[1]

(Ratified by: Brazil, Costa Rica, Cuba, Dominican Republic, Ecuador, Guatemala, Haiti, Honduras, Nicaragua, Panama, Paraguay, Peru, United States, and Uruguay.)

(Denounced by: Costa Rica, Guatemala, Honduras, and Nicaragua.)

Article I.

Las Naciones signatarias adoptan esta Convención para la protección de las Marcas de Fábrica y de Comercio, y Nombres Comerciales.

The signatory Nations enter into this Convention for the protection of trade-marks and commercial names.

Article II.

Toda marca debidamente registrada en uno de los Estados signatarios se considerará registrada también en los demás países de la Unión sin perjuicio de los derechos de un tercero y de los preceptos de la legislación interna de cada Nación.

Para gozar de este beneficio, deberá el industrial o comerciante interesado en el registro de la marca, contribuir, además de los derechos o emolumentos fijados en la legislación interna, con la suma de $50 (dollars) por una sola vez, que se destinará a cubrir los gastos de Registro Internacional de la respectiva Oficina.

Any mark duly registered in one of the signatory States shall be considered as registered also in the other States of the Union, without prejudice to the rights of third persons and to the provisions of the laws of each State governing the same.

In order to enjoy the benefit of the foregoing, the manufacturer or merchant interested in the registry of the mark must pay, in addition to the fees or charges fixed by the laws of the State in which application for registration is first made, the sum of fifty dollars gold, which sum shall cover all the expenses of both Bureaus for the international registration in all the signatory States.

[1] The text is taken from 39 Stat. at L. Pt. 2, p. 1675

Article III.

El depósito de una Marca de Fábrica o de Comercio en uno de los Estados signatarios, crea a favor del depositante un derecho de prioridad durante un plazo de seis meses, con el fin de que pueda hacer el depósito en los otros Estados.

En consecuencia el depósito hecho posteriormente antes del vencimiento de ese plazo, no podrá anularse por actos ejecutados en el intervalo, especialmente por otro depósito, por la publicación o el uso de la marca.

The deposit of a trade-mark in one of the signatory States produces in favor of the depositor a right of priority for the period of six months, so as to enable the depositor to make the deposit in the other States.

Therefore, the deposit made subsequently and prior to the expiration of this period, cannot be annulled by acts performed in the interval, especially by another deposit, by publication, or by the use of the mark.

Article IV.

Se considera Marca de Comercio o de Fábrica, todo signo, emblema o nombre especial que los comerciantes o industriales adopten o apliquen en sus artículos o productos para distinguirlos de los de otros industriales o comerciantes que fabriquen o negocien en artículos de la misma especie.

The following shall be considered as trade-mark: any sign, emblem, or especial name that merchants or manufacturers may adopt or apply to their goods or products in order to distinguish them from those of other manufacturers or merchants who manufacture or deal in articles of the same kind.

Article V.

No podrán adoptarse o usarse como Marca de Fábrica o de Comercio las bandaras o escudos nacionales, provinciales o municipales; las figuras inmorales o escandalosas; los distintivos que se hayan ya obtenido por otros o que den lugar a confusión con otras marcas; las denominaciones generales de artículos; los retratos o nombres de personas, sin su permiso; y cualquier dibujo que haya sido adoptado como emblema por alguna asociación fraternal o humanitaria.

The following cannot be adopted or used as trade-mark: national, provincial or municipal flags or coats-of-arms; immoral or scandalous figures; distinctive marks which may have been obtained by others or which may give rise to confusion with other marks; the general classification of articles; pictures or names of persons, without their permission; and any design which may have been adopted as an emblem by any fraternal or humanitarian association.

El precepto anterior se entenderá sin perjucio de lo que disponga la legislación interna de cada país.

The foregoing provisions shall be construed without prejudice to the particular provisions of the laws of each State.

ARTICLE VI.

Las cuestiones que se susciten sobre prioridad del depósito o adopción de una Marca de Comercio o de Fábrica, se resolverán teniendo en cuenta la fecha del depósito en el país en que se hizo la primera solicitud.

All questions which may arise regarding the priority of the deposit, or the adoption of a trade-mark, shall be decided with due regard to the date of the deposit in the State in which the first application was made therefor.

ARTICLE VII.

La propiedad de una Marca de Comercio o de Fábrica comprende la facultad de gozar de los beneficios de la misma, y el derecho de ceder su propiedad o su uso, total o parcialmente, de conformidad con la legislación interna.

The ownership of a trade-mark includes the right to enjoy the benefits thereof, and the right of assignment or transfer in whole or in part of its ownership or its use in accordance with the provisions of the laws of the respective States.

ARTICLE VIII.

La falsificación, simulación o uso indebido de una Marca de Comercio o de Fábrica, así como la falsa indicación de procedencia de un producto, será perseguida por la parte interesada, de acuerdo con las leyes del Estado en cuyo territorio se haya cometido el delito.

Se considera como parte interesada, para los efectos de este artículo, cualquier productor, fabricante o comerciante dedicado a la producción, fabricación o comercio de dicho producto, o en el caso de falsa indicación de procedencia, el establecido en la localidad falsamente indicada como de procedencia, o en la región en que dicha localidad esté situada.

The falsification, imitation or unauthorized use of a trade-mark, as also the false representation as to the origin of a product, shall be prosecuted by the interested party in accordance with the laws of the State wherein the offence is committed.

For the effects of this article, interested parties shall be understood to be any producer, manufacturer or merchant engaged in the production, manufacture or traffic of said product, or in the case of false representation of origin, one doing business in the locality falsely indicated as that of origin, or in the territory which said locality is situated.

ARTICLE IX.

Cualquier persona de uno de los Estados signatarios podrá pedir y obtener, en cualquiera de los otros Estados, ante la autoridad judicial competente, la anulación del registro de una Marca de Comercio o de Fábrica, cuando haya solicitado el registro de dicha Marca o de otra cualquiera que se pueda confundir en dicho Estado con aquella cuya anulación interese, probando:

(*a*) que la Marca, cuyo registro solicita, ha sido empleada o usada dentro del país con anterioridad al empleo o uso de la Marca registrada por el registrante, o por aquel o aquellos de quienes él la hubo;

(*b*) que el registrante de la Marca cuya anulación se pretende, tuviera conocimiento de la propiedad, empleo o uso de la Marca del solicitante en cualquiera de los Estados signatarios, con anterioridad al empleo o uso de la Marca registrada por el registrante, o por aquél o aquéllos de quienes él la hubo;

(*c*) que el registrante no tenía derecho a la propiedad, uso o empleo, de la Marca registrada, en la fecha de su depósito;

(*d*) que la Marca registrada no hubiera sido usada o empleada por el registrante o su causahabiente, dentro del plazo que marquen las leyes del Estado en que se haya verificado el registro.

Any person in any of the signatory States shall have the right to petition and obtain in any of the States, through its competent judicial authority, the annullment of the registration of a trade-mark, when he shall have made application for the registration of that mark, or of any other mark calculated to be confused, in such State, with the mark in whose annullment he is interested, upon proving:

(*a*) That the mark, the registration whereof he solicits, has been employed or used within the country prior to the employment or use of the mark registered by the person registering it, or by the persons from whom he has derived title;

(*b*) That the registrant had knowledge of the ownership, employment or use in any of the signatory States, of the mark of the applicant, the annullment whereof is sought, prior to the use of the registered mark by the registrant or by those from whom he has derived title;

(*c*) That the registrant had no right to the ownership, employment or use of the registered mark on the date of its deposit;

(*d*) That the registered mark had not been used or employed by the registrant or by his assigns within the term fixed by the laws of the State in which the registration shall have been made.

Article X.

Los nombres comerciales serán protegidos en todos los Estados de la Unión, sin obligación de depósito o registro, formen o no parte de una Marca de Fábrica o de Comercio.

Commercial names shall be protected in all the States of the Union, without deposit or registration, whether the same form part of a trade-mark or not.

Article XI.

A los fines indicados en el presente Tratado se constituye una Unión de las Naciones Americanas que funcionará por medio de dos Oficinas establecidas, una en la ciudad de la Habana y otra en la de Río Janeiro, en completa correlación entre sí.

For the purposes indicated in the present Convention a Union of American Nations is hereby constituted, which shall act through two International Bureaus established one in the city of Havana, Cuba, and the other in the city of Rio de Janeiro, Brazil, acting in complete accord with each other.

Article XII.

Las Oficinas Internacionales tendrán las siguientes funciones:

1. Llevar un registro de los certificados de propiedad de Marcas de Fábrica y de Comercio, que se expidan por algunos de los Estados signatarios.

2. Reunir cuantos informes y datos tengan relación con la protección de la propiedad intelectual e industrial, y publicarlos y circularlos en las Naciones de la Unión, así como suministrarles cualquier información especial que necesiten sobre la materia.

3. Fomentar el estudio y divulgación de las cuestiones relativas a la protección de la propiedad intelectual e industrial, publicando al efecto una o más revistas oficiales, en las cuales se insertarán, en su totalidad o en resumen, los

The International Bureaus shall have the following duties:

1. To keep a register of the certificate of ownership of trademarks issued by any of the signatory States.

2. To collect such reports and data as relate to the protection of intellectual and industrial property and to publish and circulate them among the Nations of the Union, as well as to furnish them whatever special information they may need upon this subject.

3. To encourage the study and publicity of the questions relating to the protection of intellectual and industrial property; to publish for this purpose one or more official reviews, containing the full texts or digest or all documents forwarded to the Bureaus by the

documentos que remitan a la Oficina las autoridades de los Estados signatarios.

Los Gobiernos de dichos Estados se comprometen a remitir a las Oficinas Internacionales Americanas las publicaciones oficiales que contengan declaraciones de registro de Marcas, nombres comerciales y concesiones de patentes, de privilegios, así como las sentencias de nulidad de Marcas o Patentes, pronunciadas por sus respectivos Tribunales.

4. Comunicar a los Gobiernos de los Estados de la Unión cualquier dificultad u obstáculo que se oponga o demore la eficaz aplicación de esta Convención.

5. Concurrir con los Gobiernos de los Estados signatarios a la preparación de Conferencias Internacionales para el estudio de legislaciones relativas a la propiedad industrial y las reformas que convenga introducir en el régimen de la Unión o en los Tratados vigentes sobre protección de aquéllas. Los Directores de la Oficinas tendrán el derecho de asistir a las sesiones de las Conferencias, con voz pero sin voto.

6. Presentar a los Gobiernos de Cuba y de los Estados Unidos del Brasil relaciones anuales de los trabajos realizados, comunicándolos al mismo tiempo a los Gobiernos de todos los demás Estados de la Unión.

7. Iniciar y mantener relaciones con Oficinas análogas y con Sociedades e Instituciones, científicas e industriales, para el canje de publicaciones, informes y datos que tiendan al

authorities of the signatory States.

The Governments of said States shall send to the International American Bureaus their official publications which contain the announcements of the registrations of trade-marks, and commercial names, and the grants of patents and privileges, as well as the judgments rendered by the respective courts concerning the invalidity of trade-marks and patents.

4. To communicate to the Governments of the Union any difficulties or obstacles that may oppose or delay the effective application of this Convention.

5. To aid the Governments of the signatory States in the preparations of international conferences for the study of legislation concerning industrial property, and to secure such alterations as it may be proper to propose in the regulations of the Union, or in treaties in force to protect industrial property. In case such conferences take place, the Directors of the Bureaus shall have the right to attend the meetings and there to express their opinions, but not to vote.

6. To present to the Governments of Cuba and of the United States of Brazil, respectively, yearly reports of their labors which shall be communicated at the same time to all the Governments of the other States of the Union.

7. To initiate and establish relations with similar Bureaus, and with the scientific and industrial associations and insti-

progreso del derecho de la propiedad industrial.

8. Investigar los casos en que las Marcas de Fábrica o de Comercio, los Dibujos o Modelos Industriales, no hayan sido reconocidos o registrados, de acuerdo con esta Convención, por autoridades de algunos de los Estados de la Unión, comunicando los hechos e informando las razones aducidas al Gobierno del país de origen y a los interesados.

9. Cooperar, como agentes de los Gobiernos de las Naciones signatarias, ante las autoridades respectivas, al mejor desempeño de cualquiera gestión que tenga por objeto promover o realizar los fines de esta Convención.

tutions for the exchange of publications, information and data conducive to the progress of the protection of industrial property.

8. To investigate cases where trade-marks, designs, and industrial models, have failed to obtain the recognition of registration provided for by this Convention, on the part of the authorities of any one of the States forming the Union, and to communicate the facts and reasons to the Government of the country of origin and to interested parties.

9. To coöperate as agents for each one of the Governments of the signatory States before the respective authorities for the better performance of any act tending to promote or accomplish the ends of this Convention.

Article XIII.

La Oficina establecida en la ciudad de la Habana, tendrá a su cargo los registros de las Marcas de Comercio y de Fábrica que procedan de los Estados Unidos de America, México, Cuba, Haití, República Dominicana, El Salvador, Honduras, Nicaragua, Costa Rica, Guatemala y Panamá.

La Oficina establecida en la ciudad de Río de Janeiro, tendrá a su cargo los registros de las Marcas de Comercio y de Fábrica que procedan del Brasil, Uruguay, Argentina, Paraguay, Bolivia, Chile, Perú, Ecuador, Venezuela y Colombia.

The Bureau established in the city of Havana, Cuba, shall have charge of the registration of trade-marks coming from the United States of America, Mexico, Cuba, Haiti, the Dominican Republic, El Salvador, Honduras, Nicaragua, Costa Rica, Guatemala, and Panama.

The Bureau established in the city of Rio de Janeiro, shall have charge of the registration of trade-marks coming from Brazil, Uruguay, the Argentine Republic, Paraguay, Bolivia, Chile, Peru, Ecuador, Venezuela, and Colombia.

Article XIV.

Las dos Oficinas Internacionales se considerarán como una sola, y a los efectos de unificación de los registros, se dispone:

(*a*) que ambas lleven los mismos libros y la misma contabilidad, bajo un idéntico sistema;

(*b*) que cada semana se remitan, recíprocamente, copias de todas las solicitudes, registros, comunicaciones y demás documentos que se refieran al reconocimiento de los derechos de los propietarios.

The two International Bureaus shall be considered as one, and for the purpose of unification of the registrations it is provided:

(*a*) Both shall have the same books and the same accounts kept under an identical system.

(*b*) Copies shall be reciprocally transmitted weekly from one to the other of all applications, registrations, communications and other documents affecting the recognition of the rights of owners of trade-marks.

Article XV.

Las Oficinas Internacionales se regirán por un mismo Reglamento, redactado de acuerdo por los Gobiernos de las Repúblicas de Cuba y los Estados Unidos del Brasil, y aprobados por todos los demás Estados signatarios.

Los presupuestos de gastos serán aprobados por dichos Gobiernos y costeados por todos los Estados signatarios, en una proporción igual a la establecida por la Oficina Internacional de las Repúblicas Americanas en Washington, y a ese respecto, esas Oficinas estarán bajo el control de los Gobiernos en cuyos países tengan su asiento.

Las Oficinas Internacionales podrán adoptar los Reglamentos interiores que crean convenientes para el cumplimiento de lo estipulado en esta Convención, siempre que no estén en contradicción con los términos de ella.

The International Bureaus shall be governed by identical regulations, formed with the concurrence of the Governments of the Republic of Cuba and of the United States of Brazil and approved by all the other signatory States.

Their budgets, after being sanctioned by the said Governments, shall be defrayed by all the signatory States in the same proportion as that established for the International Bureau of the American Republics at Washington, and in this particular they shall be placed under the control of those Governments within whose territories they are established.

The International Bureaus may establish such rules of practice and procedure, not inconsistent with the terms of this Convention, as they may deem necessary and proper to give effect to its provisions.

ARTICLE XVI.

Los Gobiernos de las Repúblicas de Cuba y de los Estados Unidos del Brasil procederán a la organización de las Oficinas de la Unión Internacional, de acuerdo con lo estipulado, tan pronto como haya sido ratificada esta Convención por las dos terceras partes, a lo menos, de las Naciones pertenecientes a cada grupo.

No será necesario el establecimiento simultáneo de las dos Oficinas, pudiendo instalarse una sola, si hubiese el número señalado de Naciones signatarias.

The Governments of the Republic of Cuba and of the United States of Brazil shall proceed with the organization of the Bureaus of the International Union as herein provided, upon the ratification of this Convention by at least two-thirds of the Nations belonging to each group.

The simultaneous establishment of both Bureaus shall not be necessary; one only may be established if there be the number of adherent governments provided for above.

ARTICLE XVII.

Los Tratados sobre Marcas de Comercio o de Fábrica, celebrados con anterioridad entre los Estados signatarios, serán substituidos por esta Convención, desde la fecha de su ratificación, en cuanto a las relaciones entre dichos Estados.

The treaties on trade-marks previously concluded by and between the signatory States, shall be substituted by the present convention from the date of its ratification, as far as the relations between the signatory States are concerned.

ARTICLE XVIII.

La ratificación o adhesiones de la Naciones Americanas a esta Convención, serán comunicadas al Gobierno de la República Argentina, que las hará saber a todos los demás Estados de la Unión. Estas comunicaciones harán las veces de canje.

The ratifications or adhesions of the American States to the present Convention shall be communicated to the Government of the Argentine Republic, which shall lay them before the other States of the Union. These communications shall take the place of an exchange of ratifications.

ARTICLE XIX.

El Estado signatario que creyere conveniente desligarse de esta Convención, lo hará saber al Gobierno de la Repúb-

Any signatory State that may see fit to withdraw from the present Convention shall so notify the Government of the

lica Argentina, que lo comunicará a los demás Estados de la Unión; y un año después de recibida la comunicación respectiva, cesará la vigencia de esta Convención respecto del Estado que la hubiere denunciado.

Argentine Republic, which shall communicate this fact to the other States of the Union, and one year after the receipt of such communication this Convention shall cease with regard to the State that shall have withdrawn.

II.

Convention for the Protection of Commercial, Industrial and Agricultural Trade Marks and Commercial Names

Signed at Santiago, Chile, April 28, 1923.[1]

(Ratified by: Brazil, Chile, Cuba, The Dominican Republic, Guatemala, Haiti, Paraguay, and the United States of America.)

Article I.

Párrafo 1. Las Altas Partes Contratantes convienen en que toda marca de fábrica, comercio o agricultura, registrada o depositada en uno de los Estados signatarios de la Convención, por persona domiciliada en cualquiera de ellos, directamente o por medio de representante legal, podrá obtener en los demás la misma protección que éstos otorguen a las marcas registradas o depositadas en su propio territorio, sin perjuicio de derechos de terceros y siempre que se llenen las formalidades y condiciones exigidas por la legislación interna de cada Estado, y se cumpla con los siguientes requisitos:

(*a*) El interesado en el registro o depósito de la marca deberá presentar a la respectiva Oficina Interamericana, por medio de la Oficina correspondiente del Estado del primer registro o depósito, una solicitud de reconocimiento de los derechos que alegue, de acuerdo con los requisitos exigidos en el Apéndice, que se declara parte integrante de esta Convención;

Section 1. The High Contracting Parties agree that any commercial, industrial, or agricultural trade-mark registered or deposited in any of the States signatory to the Convention, by a person domiciled in any of such States, either directly, or through his duly authorized representative, may obtain in the other signatory States the same protection granted by them to the marks registered or deposited in their own territory, without prejudice to the rights of third parties, and provided that the formalities and conditions required by the domestic law of each State, as well as the following requirements, are complied with:

(*a*) Any person interested in the registration or deposit of the mark shall present to the proper Inter American Bureau through the proper office of the State of first registration or deposit, an application for recognition of the rights claimed, in accordance with the requirements prescribed in the Appendix of this Convention, which is

[1] The text is taken from *United States Treaty Series*, No. 751.

(*b*) Pagará, además de los derechos o emolumentos fijados por la legislación interna de cada Estado en que solicite el reconocimiento de sus derechos, y los otros gastos que este reconocimiento origine, una suma equivalente a cincuenta dólares oro americano por una sola vez en cada período, y por una misma marca, que se destinará a cubrir los gastos de la respectiva Oficina Interamericana.

PÁRRAFO 2. El período durante el cual se otorgue protección será el mismo que acuerden a las marcas las leyes del respectivo Estado.

PÁRRAFO 3. Al fin de cada período podrá renovarse en cada Estado la protección que otorga esta Convención, previo cumplimiento de los requisitos establecidos en el inciso (*b*) de este artículo. El interesado podrá también presentar directamente a la respectiva Oficina Interamericana la solicitud de renovación.

PÁRRAFO 4. Los nombres comerciales, formen o no parte de una marca, serán protegidos, con arreglo a la ley interna de cada Estado, en todos los Estados signatarios, sin obligación de depósito o registro.

declared to be a part hereof.

(*b*) He shall pay, besides the fees or charges established by the domestic legislation of each State in which recognition of rights is desired, and other expenses incident to such recognition, a fee equivalent in value to fifty dollars ($50.00) United States gold, this sum to be paid only once for each period and for a single mark. Such fee shall be used to cover the expenses of the said Inter American Bureau.

SECTION 2. The period during which protection is granted shall be the same as that accorded by the laws of the particular State.

SECTION 3. Protection under this Convention may be renewed at the expiration of each period upon fulfillment of the requirements set forth in paragraph (*b*) hereof. Application for renewal may also be made by the interested party directly to the proper Inter American Bureau.

SECTION 4. Commercial names shall be protected in all the signatory States, without deposit or registration, whether the same form part of a trademark or not, in accordance with the domestic law of each State.

ARTICLE II.

La fecha de presentación en el país en que se haga la primera solicitud para el registro o depósito mediante la Oficina Interamericana respectiva, determinará, a falta de otros medios de prueba de la propiedad de la marca, la prioridad para el reg-

The date of filing in the State where first application is made for registration or deposit through the proper Inter American Bureau, in the absence of other proof of ownership of a mark, shall determine priority for the registration or deposit

istro o depósito en cualquiera de los Estado contratantes.

of such mark in any of the signatory States.

ARTICLE III.

PÁRRAFO 1. Los Estados contratantes, immediatamente que reciban una solicitud de reconocimiento remitida por la Oficina Interamericana respectiva, determinarán conforme a sus propias leyes si puede concederse la protección, y notificarán su resolución a la misma Oficina Interamericana a la mayor brevedad posible.

PÁRRAFO 2. En caso de oposición al registro o depósito de una marca conforme a esta Convención, el plazo para contestarla dentro del Estado en que se formule, emperzará a correr noventa días después de remitido el aviso de la oposición a la Oficina Interamericana respectiva, la cual no tendrá otra intervención en el proceso a que dé lugar la oposición.

SECTION 1. Each signatory State, upon receipt of an application for recognition communicated by the proper Inter American Bureau, shall determine whether protection can be granted in accordance with its laws, and notify the Inter American Bureau as soon as possible of its decision.

SECTION 2. In case objection is made to the registration or deposit of a mark under this Convention, the term to answer such objection in the country where it is made shall begin ninety days after the date of sending notice of such objection to the proper Inter American Bureau. This Bureau shall have no other part in the controversy originated by the opposition.

ARTICLE IV.

La transferencia de marca registrada o depositada en uno de los Estados contratantes será reconocida igualmente en cada uno de los otros Estados, con la misma fuerza y efectos que si se hubiese efectuado conforme a sus leyes respectivas, siempre que se trate de una marca que haya sido registrada o depositada en el Estado en que se solicite el reconocimiento de la transferencia conforme a esta Convención, y mientras no se contrarien las bases del Artículo V de esta Convención. Se notificará la transferencia por medio de la Administración del Estado

The transfer of a mark registered or deposited in one of the contracting States shall be equally recognized in each one of the other States with the same force and effect as if made in accordance with the respective laws of each one of those States, provided that the mark transferred is a mark registered or deposited in the country where the recognition of transference under this Convention is applied for, and, provided that the principles of Article V of this Convention are not impaired. Notification of transfer shall be made through the

del primer registro o depósito y de la respectiva Oficina Interamericana, previo pago de los derechos que correspondan en cada Estado por dicha transferencia.

proper office of the State of first registration or deposit and the proper Inter American Bureau, upon payment of the fees corresponding to each State for such transference.

ARTICLE V.

PÁRRAFO 1. En toda cuestión de índole civil, criminal o administrativa que se suscite en un Estado con respecto a una marca, tal como oposición, falsificación, simulación o apropiación indebida, así como la falsa indicación de procedencia de un producto, sólo serán competentes las autoridades de ese mismo Estado, con sujeción a sus propias leyes.

PÁRRAFO 2. Cuando al propietario de una marca que pida el reconocimiento de derechos conforme a esta Convención, se le niegue en uno de los Estados signatarios la protección que esta Convención concede, y esa negativa se base en un registro previo o en una solicitud pendiente, el propietario tendrá derecho a solicitar la cancelación de la marca registrada anteriormente y a obtener dicha cancelación, si probare, conforme a los procedimientos legales del Estado en que se solicite la cancelación, esa negativa y, además, lo siguiente:

(*a*) Que gozaba de protección legal para su marca en uno de los Estados signatarios antes de la fecha de la solicitud del registro que trata de anular; o

(*b*) Que el registrador no tenía derecho a la propiedad, uso o empleo de la marca registrada en la fecha de su depósito; o

SECTION 1. In any civil, criminal, or administrative proceeding arising in a country with respect to a mark, such as opposition, falsification, imitation, or unauthorized appropriation, as also the false representation as to the origin of a product, the domestic authorities of the same State alone shall have jurisdiction thereof, and the precepts of law and procedure of that State shall be observed.

SECTION 2. When refused protection under this Convention in a signatory State because of prior registration or a pending application for registration, the proprietor of a mark claiming recognition of rights under this Convention shall have the right to seek and obtain the cancellation of the previously registered mark, upon proving, according to the procedure by law of the country where cancellation is sought, such refusal, and either:

(*a*) That he had legal protection for his mark in any of the contracting States before the date of application for the registration which he seeks to cancel; or

(*b*) That the registrant had no right to the ownership, use, or employment of the registered mark at the date of its deposit; or

(*c*) Que ha sido abandonada la marca protegida por el registro cuya cancelación solicita.

PÁRRAFO 3 (transitorio). Los que hayan solicitado los beneficios de esta Convención para sus marcas y no hayan obtenido protección en algunos Estados podrán aprovecharse del derecho establecido en este Artículo dentro del plazo de dos años, contados desde la fecha en que esta Convención reformada entre en vigor. Los que soliciten dichos beneficios posteriormente podrán hacer valer este derecho dentro del término de un año contado, en cada caso, desde el día siguiente a la fecha en que la Oficina Interamericana respectiva reciba el aviso de denegación de la protección.

PÁRRAFO 4. No serán objeto de este recurso las marcas cuyo registro o depósito sea ya inatacable, según la ley nacional; pero podrán serlo las renovaciones.

PÁRRAFO 5. La comprobación de que una marca de fábrica encubre o simula la calidad, naturaleza o procedenica reales de la mercadería que protege, es causa de anulación del registro o depósito efectuado por medio de la Oficina Interamericana correspondiente.

(*c*) That the mark covered by the registration which he seeks to cancel has been abandoned.

SECTION 3 (transitory). Those who have heretofore sought the benefits of this Convention for their marks and who have been denied protection in certain States, may avail themselves of the right established in this article within two years after the present revision enters into effect. Those who subsequently seek to secure the benefits of the Convention shall have a period of one year, calculated in each instance from the day following that of the receipt by the proper Inter American Bureau of notice of refusal of protection, within which they may avail themselves of this right.

SECTION 4. This recourse shall not be applicable to trademarks the registration or deposit of which is already beyond question under the national legislation; but it shall apply to renewals.

SECTION 5. The proof that a trade-mark conceals or misrepresents the true quality, nature, or origin of the merchandise covered by it, shall be cause for cancellation of the registration or deposit effected through the respective Inter American Bureau.

ARTICLE VI.

Para los fines indicados en la presente Convención, se constituye una Unión de las Naciones Americanas que funcionará por medio de dos Oficinas Interamericanas, establecidas, una

For the purposes indicated in the present Convention, a Union of American Nations is hereby constituted which shall act through two International Bureaus, established, one in the

en la ciudad de la Habana y otra en la de Río de Janeiro.

city of Havana, and the other in the city of Rio de Janeiro.

ARTICLE VII.

Las Altas Partes Contratantes convienen en otorgar franqueo libre a la correspondencia oficial de las Oficinas.

The High Contracting Parties agree to confer the postal frank on the official correspondence of the Bureaus.

ARTICLE VIII.

Las Oficinas Intermaericanas para el registro de marcas tendrán las siguientes funciones:

PÁRRAFO 1. Llevar nota circunstanciada de las solicitudes de reconocimiento de marcas que reciban por medio de las oficinas nacionales y tramiten para los efectos de esta Convención, así como de las transferencias y demás datos que a dichas marcas se refieran.

PÁRRAFO 2. Comunicar a cada uno de los Estados contratantes, las solicitudes de reconocimiento recibidas, para los efectos que correspondan.

PÁRRAFO 3. Distribuir las cuotas que reciban, en conformidad a lo prescrito en el inciso (*b*) del Artículo I.

Las Oficinas Interamericanas harán a los respectivos Gobiernos o a sus Agentes debidamente autorizados en la Habana y en Río de Janeiro, si aquellos así lo resolvieren, los pagos estipulados, al tiempo de pedir el reconocimiento de los derechos alegados por el solicitante conforme a esta Convención. El costo de la remesa de dichos pagos será de cuenta del Estado a quien se haga. La Oficinas Interamericanas harán llegar a

The Inter American Bureaus for the registration of trademarks shall have the following duties:

SECTION 1. To keep a detailed record of the applications for the recognition of marks received through the national offices of registration and to which they give course for the purposes of this Convention, as well as of all assignments or transfers thereof and of all notices pertaining thereto.

SECTION 2. To communicate to each of the contracting States, for such action as may be necessary, the applications for recognition received.

SECTION 3. To distribute the fees received, in accordance with the provisions of paragraph (*b*), Article I.

The Inter American Bureaus shall remit to the proper governments or, if the governments should so desire, to their local representatives in Havana and at Rio de Janeiro, duly authorized therefor, the charges stipulated at the time when recognition of the alleged rights is requested by the applicant in accordance with this Convention. The cost of remitting the

los interesados las sumas que les sean devueltas.

PÁRRAFO 4. Comunicar al Estado de primer registro o depósito para conocimiento del propietario de la marca, los avisos recibidos de los otros Estados, con respecto a la concesión, oposición o denegación de protección, o cualquiera otra circunstancia que se relacione con la marca.

PÁRRAFO 5. Publicar periódicamente boletines en que se dé noticia de las solicitudes de protección conforme a esta Convención recibidas de los distintos Estados y remitidas a ellos conforme a los preceptos de la Convención, así como documentos, informes, estudios y artículos sobre protectión de la propiedad industrial.

Las Altas Partes Contratantes convienen en proporcionar a las Oficinas Interamericanas todas las gacetas, revistas y otras publicaciones oficiales que contengan noticias de registro de marcas de fábrica y nombres comerciales, así como de las actuaciones judiciales y resoluciones relacionadas con esta materia.

PÁRRAFO 6. Llevar a efecto toda investigación que el Gobierno de cualquiera de los Estados signatarios les pida sobre esta materia, y fomentar el estudio de problemas, dificultades u obstáculos que entorpezcan el funcionamiento de la Convención.

PÁRRAFO 7. Cooperar con los Gobiernos de los Estados contratantes en la preparación del material para conferencias inter-

said charges shall be for account of the States to which remittance is made. The Inter American Bureaus shall return to the interested parties any sums returned to such Bureaus.

SECTION 4. To communicate to the State of first registration or deposit, for the information of the owner of the mark, the notices received from other countries with respect to the granting, opposition to, or denial of protection or any other circumstance related to the mark.

SECTION 5. To publish periodical bulletins in which shall appear notices of applications for protection in accordance with this Convention received from and sent to the various States under the provisions of the Convention, as well as documents, informations, studies, and articles concerning protection of industrial property.

The High Contracting Parties agree to furnish to the Inter American Bureaus all the official gazettes, reviews, and other publications containing notices of the registration of trademarks and commercial names, as well as of judicial proceedings and decisions relative thereto.

SECTION 6. To carry on any investigation on the subject of trade-marks which the government of any of the signatory States may request, and to encourage the investigation of problems, difficulties or obstacles which may hinder the operation of this Convention.

SECTION 7. To coöperate with the governments of the contracting States in the prepara-

nacionales sobre esta materia; presentar a dichos Estados las indicaciones que estimen útiles y las opiniones que se les soliciten sobre las modificaciones que deban introducirse en la presente Convención o las leyes que afecten la propieded industrial; y, en general, facilitar la realización de los fines de esta Convención.

PÁRRAFO 8. Dar cuenta a los Gobiernos contratantes, por lo menos una vez al año, de los trabajos realizados por las Oficinas.

PÁRRAFO 9. Mantener relaciones con oficinas análogas, con sociedades y organizaciones científicas e industriales, para el canje de publicaciones, informes y datos que tiendan al progreso del derecho de la propiedad industrial.

PÁRRAFO 10. Establecer, de acuerdo con las estipulaciones de esta Convención, los preceptos que los Directores estimen necesarios para el manejo interno de las Oficinas.

tion of material for international conferences on this subject; to present to the said States such suggestions as they may consider useful, and such opinions as may be requested as to what modifications should be introduced in the present Convention or in the laws concerning industrial property; and in general to facilitate the execution of the purposes of this Convention.

SECTION 8. To inform the signatory governments at least once a year as to the work which the Bureaus are doing.

SECTION 9. To maintain relations with similar offices and scientific and industrial institutions and organizations for the exchange of publications, information, and data relative to the progress of the law of industrial property.

SECTION 10. To establish, in accordance with the provisions of this Convention, the regulations which the Directors may consider necessary for the internal administration of the Bureaus.

ARTICLE IX.

La Oficina establecida en la ciudad de la Habana gestionará ante los Estados contratantes el registro o depósito de las marcas de comercio, de fábrica y de agricultura que procedan de los Estados Unidos de América, Cuba, Haití, República Dominicana, Guatemala, El Salvador, Honduras, Nicaragua, Costa Rica, Panamá, Colombia y Ecuador.

La Oficina establecida en la

The Bureau established in the city of Havana shall arrange with the contracting States for the registration or deposit of commercial, industrial, and agricultural trade-marks coming from the United States of America, Cuba, Haiti, Dominican Republic, Guatemala, El Salvador, Honduras, Nicaragua, Costa Rica, Panama, Colombia, and Ecuador.

The Bureau established in

ciudad de Río de Janeiro, gestionará el registro de las marcas que procedan de Brasil, Uruguay, la República Argentina, Paraguay, Chile y Venezuela.

PÁRRAFO TRANSITORIO. La Oficina Interamericana de Río de Janeiro se instalará tan pronto como la presente Convención haya sido ratificada por un tercio de los Estados signatarios.

Rio de Janeiro shall arrange for the registration of the marks coming from Brazil, Uruguay, the Argentine Republic, Paraguay, Chile, and Venezuela.

Transitory paragraph. — The Inter American Bureau of Rio de Janeiro shall be installed as soon as the present Convention shall have been ratified by one-third of the signatory States.

ARTICLE X.

Las dos Oficinas Interamericanas se considerarán como una sola y, con el objeto de uniformar sus procedimientos, se dispone:

(*a*) Que ambas adopten un mismo sistema de libros y de contabilidad;

(*b*) Que se remitan, recíprocamente, copias de todas las solicitudes, registros, comunicaciones y demás documentos que se refieran al reconocimiento de los derechos de los propietarios de marcas.

The two Inter American Bureaus shall be considered as one, and for the purposes of uniformity in their procedure, it is provided:

(*a*) That both Bureaus adopt the same system of books and of accounts.

(*b*) That each of them send to the other copies of all applications, registrations, communications and other documents relative to the recognition of the rights of owners of marks.

ARTICLE XI.

La Oficinas Interamericanas se regirán por un mismo Reglamento, redactado de acuerdo entre los Gobiernos de la República de Cuba y de los Estados Unidos del Brasil.

The Inter American Bureaus shall both be governed by the same regulations, prepared for the purpose by the governments of the Republics of Cuba and of Brazil.

ARTICLE XII.

Se dedicará al costo del sostenimiento y funcionamiento de cada Oficina Interamericana la parte de los derechos recibidos por la misma destinados este propósito, conforme a lo determinado en esta Convención, y el producto de la venta de sus publicaciones a particulares; y si esas sumas no bastaren, el

That part of the fees received by each Inter American Bureau which is stipulated for this purpose by the provisions of this Convention, shall be assigned to the maintenance and operation thereof.

The proceeds of the sale of publications by the Inter American Bureaus to individuals shall

exceso del costo será pagado por los Estados contratantes en la forma siguiente:

El déficit total del presupuesto de funcionamiento de ambas Oficinas será cubierto en un ochenta por ciento por los Estados contratantes en proporción al número de marcas que anualmente hayan hecho registrar por medio de las Oficinas Interamericanas, y el veinte por ciento restante, por los mismos Estados, en proporción al número de marcas que hayan registrado a pedido de las Oficinas Interamericanas.

El saldo sobrante anual que hubiere en una Oficina, se aplicará a disminuir el déficit que pudiera haber en la otra.

Las Oficinas Interamericanas no incurrirán en gasto o compromiso alguno que no aparezca en sus presupuestos definitivos y para el cual no existan fondos disponibles en la época en que hubiera de incurrirse en dicho gasto o compromiso.

El presupuesto provisional de gastos anuales de cada una de las Oficinas se someterá a la aprobación del Gobierno del país en que tenga su sede, y se comunicará a los Estados contratantes para las observaciones que juzguen conveniente hacer.

La fiscalización de las cuentas de las Oficinas Interamericanas la hará el funcionario autorizado por el respectivo Gobierno, y su informe lo remitirán los Directores de las Oficinas a los Estados contratantes, por la vía diplomática.

be assigned to the same purpose; and if both these sums should be insufficient, the deficit shall be paid by the contracting States in the following manner:

80% of the total deficit of the operating budget of both Bureaus shall be paid by the contracting States in proportion to the number of marks which they may have had registered each year through the Inter American Bureaus, and the balance of 20% by the same States in proportion to the number of marks they may have registered at the request of the Inter American Bureaus.

Any annual surplus in one of the Bureaus shall be assigned to the reduction of the deficit, if any, of the other.

The Inter American Bureaus shall not incur any expense or obligation which does not appear in their definite budgets and for which no funds may have been made available at the time of incurring such expense or obligation.

The provisional budget of annual expenditures of each Bureau shall be submitted to the approval of the Government of the State in which such Bureau is established, and shall be communicated to the contracting States for such observations as they may see fit to formulate.

The auditing of the accounts of the Inter American Bureaus shall be done by the officer authorized by the respective government, and the Directors of the Bureaus shall transmit the auditor's report to the contracting States through diplomatic channels.

Article XIII.

Las marcas que gocen de la protección de la Convención de 1910 continuarán siendo protegidas sin pago de derecho alguno a los Estados contratantes.

Las Altas Partes Contratantes convienen en continuar otorgando la protección de sus leyes de acuerdo con la Convención de 1910, si la hubieren ratificado, a todas las marcas que se reciban hasta el día en que rija en ellas la Convención reformada.

Trade-marks which enjoy the protection of the Convention of 1910 shall continue to enjoy this protection without payment of any fees to the contracting States.

The High Contracting Parties agree that the protection accorded by their national legislation to all marks received up to the day on which the revised Convention becomes effective shall continue to be granted in accordance with the Convention of 1910, if they have ratified it.

Article XIV.

Las ratificaciones o adhesiones a esta Convención serán comunicadas al Gobierno de la República de Chile, el cual las hará saber a los demás Estados signatarios o adherentes. Estas comunicaciones harán las veces de canje de ratificaciones. La Convención reformada entrará en vigor treinta días después de que reciba el Gobierno de Chile aviso de su ratificación por un número de Estados que constituya un tercio de los Estados signatarios; y desde ese momento cesará la Convención firmada el 20 de agosto de 1910, sin perjuicio de lo que se previene en el Artículo XIII de la presente Convención.

El Gobierno de Chile se compromete a notificar, por las vías telegráfica y postal, a todos los Estados signatarios y adherentes, la fecha en que la Convención en su forma actual entre en vigor conforme a lo prevenido en este artículo.

The ratifications or adhesions to this Convention shall be communicated to the Government of the Republic of Chile, which shall communicate them to the other signatory or adhering States. These communications shall take the place of an exchange of ratifications.

The revised Convention shall become effective thirty days after the receipt by the Government of Chile of notice of ratification by a number of countries equivalent to one-third of the signatory States, and from that moment the Convention signed on August 20, 1910, shall cease to exist, without prejudice to the provisions of Article XIII of this Convention.

The Government of Chile obligates itself to communicate by telegram and in writing to all the signatory and adhering States the date on which the Convention in its present form becomes effective in accordance with the provisions of this Article.

Article XV.

Los Estados americanos que no han estado representados en esta Conferencia podrán adherirse a esta Convención comunicando su decisión en debida forma al Gobierno de la República de Chile, debiendo ser incorporados al grupo a que deseen pertenecer.

The American States not represented in this Conference may adhere to this Convention by communicating their decision in due form to the Government of the Republic of Chile, and shall be assigned to the group which each may select.

Article XVI.

El Estado contratante que creyere conveniente desligarse de esta Convención lo hará saber al Gobierno de la República de Chile, el cual lo comunicará a los demás Estados signatarios; y, un año después de recibida la comunicación respectiva, cesará la vigencia de esta Convención respecto del Estado que la hubiere denunciado; pero esta denuncia no afectará los derechos previamente adquiridos conforme a esta Convención.

Any signatory State that may see fit to withdraw from this Convention shall so notify the Government of the Republic of Chile, which shall communicate the fact to the other signatory States; and one year after the receipt of such notification this Convention shall cease in respect of the State that shall have withdrawn, but such withdrawal shall not affect the rights previously acquired in accordance with this Convention.

Article XVII.

Las Oficinas Interamericanas continuarán funcionando mientras permanezcan adheridos a la Convención no menos de la mitad de los Estados ratificantes. Si el número de Estados adherentes a la Convención se redujere a menos de la mitad, se liquidarán las Oficinas bajo la dirección de los Gobiernos de Cuba y del Brasil, y se distribuirán sus fondos entre los Estados adherentes en la misma proporción en que ellos, en su caso, hubieran de contribuir para sostenerla. Los edificios y otras propiedades materiales de las Oficinas pasarán a ser propiedad

The Inter American Bureaus shall continue so long as not less than one-half of the ratifying States adhere to the Convention. If the number of States adhering to the Convention shall become less than half, the Bureaus shall be liquidated under the direction of the Governments of Cuba and Brazil, and their funds shall be distributed among the adhering countries in the same proportion as they would have contributed to their support. The buildings and other tangible property of the Bureaus shall become the property of the Governments of

de los Gobiernos de Cuba y del Brasil, respectivamente, en reconocimiento de los servicios de esas Repúblicas para llevar a la práctica la Convención; pero dichos Gobiernos se comprometen a dedicar esas propiedades a objetos de carácter esencialmente interamericano.

Las Altas Partes Contratantes convienen en aceptar como definitiva toda disposición que se tome para la liquidación de las Oficinas.

La terminación de la Convención no afectará los derechos adquiridos durante el tiempo en que haya estado en vigor.

Cuba and Brazil, respectively, in recognition of the services of those Republics in giving effect to the Convention, it being understood that the said Governments shall dedicate such property to purposes pre-eminently inter American in character.

The High Contracting Parties agree to accept as final any steps which may be taken for the liquidation of the Bureaus.

The termination of the Convention shall not affect rights acquired during the period of its effectiveness.

Article XVIII.

Las diferencias entre los Estados Contratantes relativas a la interpretación o ejecución de esta Convención, se decidirán por arbitraje.

Any differences between the contracting States relative to the interpretation or execution of this Convention shall be decided by arbitration.

III.

International Convention for the Protection of Industrial Property.[1]

(Signed at The Hague, November 6, 1925.)

Article 1.

Les pays contractants sont constitués à l'état d'Union pour la protection de la propriété industrielle.

La protection de la propriété industrielle a pour objet les brevets d'invention, les modèles d'utilité, les dessins ou modèles industriels, les marques de fabrique ou de commerce, le nom commercial et les indications de provenance ou appellations d'origine, ainsi que la répression de la concurrence déloyale.

La propriété industrielle s'entend dans l'acception la plus large, et s'applique non seulement à l'industrie et au commerce proprement dits, mais également au domaine des industries agricoles (vins, grains, feuilles de tabac, fruits, bestiaux, etc.) et extractives (minéraux, eaux minérales, etc.).

Parmi les brevets d'invention sont comprises les diverses espèces de brevets industriels admises par les législations des pays contractants, telles que brevets d'importation, brevets de perfectionnement, brevets et certificats d'addition, etc.

The contracting countries constitute themselves into a Union for the protection of industrial property.

The protection of industrial property is concerned with patents, utility models, industrial designs and models, trade marks, trade names and indications of source or appellations of origin, and the repression of unfair competition.

Industrial property is to be understood in the broadest sense and applies not only to industry and commerce properly so called, but likewise to agricultural industries (wines, corn, tobacco leaves, fruit, cattle, etc.) and extractive industries (minerals, mineral waters, etc.).

Under the term "patents" are included the various kinds of industrial patents recognised by the laws of the contracting countries, such as patents of importation, patents of improvement, patents and certificates of addition, etc.

[1] The original language of the Convention is the French. The English translation is taken from the British Treaty Series, No. 16 (1928). The French text is taken from *Actes de la Conférence de la Hage de l'Union pour la Protection de la Propriété Industrielle*, Berne, 1926, p. 604.

ARTICLE 2.

Les ressortissants de chacun des pays contractants jouiront dans tous les autres pays de l'Union, en ce qui concerne la protection de la propriété industrielle, des avantages que les lois respectives accordent actuellement ou accorderont par la suite aux nationaux, le tout sans préjudice des droits spécialement prévus par la présente Convention. En conséquence, ils auront la même protection que ceux-ci et le même recours légal contre toute atteinte portée à leurs droits, sous réserve de l'accomplissement des conditions et formalités imposées aux nationaux.

Toutefois, aucune condition de domicile ou d'établissement dans le pays où la protection est réclamée ne peut être exigée des ressortissants de l'Union, pour la jouissance d'aucun des droits de propriété industrielle.

Sont expressément réservées les dispositions de la législation de chacun des pays contractants relatives à la procédure judiciaire et administrative et à la compétence, ainsi qu'a l'élection de domicile ou à la constitution d'un mandataire, qui seraient requises par les lois sur la propriété industrielle.

Persons within the jurisdiction of each of the contracting countries shall, as regards the protection of industrial property, enjoy in all the other countries of the Union the advantages that their respective laws now grant, or may hereafter grant, to their nationals, without prejudice to the rights specially provided by the present Convention. Consequently they shall have the same protection as the latter, and the same legal remedy against any infringement of their rights, provided they observe the conditions and formalities imposed on nationals.

Nevertheless, no condition as to the possession of a domicile or establishment in the country where protection is claimed may be required of persons entitled to the benefits of the Union for the enjoyment of any industrial property rights.

The provisions of the laws of each of the contracting countries relative to judicial and administrative procedure and competence, and to the choice of domicile or the authorization of an agent which may be required by the laws of industrial property, are expressly reserved.

ARTICLE 3.

Sont assimilés aux ressortissants des pays contractants les ressortissants des pays ne faisant pas partie de l'Union, qui sont domiciliés ou ont des établissements industriels ou commerciaux effectifs et sérieux sur le

Persons within the jurisdiction of countries not forming part of the Union, who are domiciled or who have real and effective industrial or commercial establishments in the territory of one of the countries of

territoire de l'un des pays de l'Union.

the Union, are assimilated to persons within the jurisdiction of the contracting countries.

ARTICLE 4.

(*a*) Celui qui aura régulièrement fait le dépôt d'une demande de brevet d'invention, d'un modèle d'utilité, d'un dessin ou modèle industriel, d'une marque de fabrique ou de commerce, dans l'un des pays contractants, ou son ayant cause, jouira, pour effectuer le dépôt dans les autres pays, et sous réserve des droits des tiers, d'un droit de priorité pendant les délais déterminés ci-après.

(*b*) En conséquence, le dépôt ultérieurement opéré dans l'un des autres pays de l'Union, avant l'expiration de ces délais ne pourra être invalidé par des faits accomplis dans l'intervalle, soit notamment, par un autre dépôt, par la publication de l'invention ou son exploitation, par la mise en vente d'exemplaires du dessin ou du modèle, par l'emploi de la marque.

(*c*) Les délais de priorité mentionnés ci-dessus seront de douze mois pour les brevets d'invention et les modèles d'utilité et de six mois pour les dessins et modèles industriels et pour les marques de fabrique ou de commerce.

Ces délais commencent à courir de la date du dépôt de la première demande dans un pays de l'Union; le jour du dépôt n'est pas compris dans le délai.

Si le dernier jour du délai est un jour férié légal dans le pays ou la protection est réclamée, le

(*a*) Any person who has duly deposited an application for a patent, or for the registration of a utility model, industrial design or model or trade mark in one of the contracting countries, or his legal representative or assignee, shall enjoy, for the purposes of deposit in the other countries, and reserving the rights of third parties, a right of priority during the periods hereinafter stated.

(*b*) Consequently, a subsequent deposit in any of the other countries of the Union before the expiration of these periods shall not be invalidated through any acts accomplished in the interval, either, for instance, by another deposit, by publication or exploitation of the invention, by the putting on sale of copies of the design or model, or by use of the mark.

(*c*) The above-mentioned periods of priority shall be twelve months for patents and utility models, and six months for industrial designs and models and trade marks.

These periods start from the date of deposit of the first application in a country of the Union; the day of deposit is not included in the period.

If the last day of the period is a *dies non* in the country where protection is claimed, the period shall be extended until the first following working day.

délai sera prorogé jusqu'au premier jour ouvrable qui suit.

(*d*) Quiconque voudra se prévaloir de la priorité d'un dépôt antérieur sera tenu de faire une déclaration indiquant la date et le pays de ce dépôt. Chaque pays déterminera à quel moment, au plus tard, cette déclaration devra être effectuée.

Ces indications seront mentionnées dans les publications émanant de l'Administration compétente, notamment sur les brevets et les descriptions y relatives.

Les pays contractants pourront exiger de celui qui fait une déclaration de priorité la production d'une copie de la demande (description, dessins, etc.) déposée antérieurement. La copie, certifiée conforme par l'Administration qui aura reçu cette demande, sera dispensée de toute légalisation, et elle pourra en tous cas être déposée à n'importe quel moment dans le délai de trois mois à dater du dépôt de la demande ultérieure. On pourra, exiger qu'elle soit accompagnée d'un certificat de la date du dépôt émanant de cette Administration et d'une traduction.

D'autres formalités ne pourront être requises pour la déclaration de priorité au moment du dépôt de la demande. Chaque pays contractant déterminera les conséquences de l'omission des formalités prévues par le présent article, sans que ces conséquences puissent excéder la perte du droit de priorité.

Ultérieurement d'autres justifications pourront être demandées.

(*d*) Any person desiring to take advantage of the priority of a previous deposit shall be bound to make a declaration giving particulars as to the date of such deposit and the country in which it was made. Each country will determine for itself the latest time at which such declaration must be made.

These particulars shall be mentioned in the publications issued by the competent authority, in particular on the patents and the specifications relating thereto.

The contracting countries may require any person making a declaration of priority to produce a copy of the application (with the specification, drawings, etc.) previously deposited. The copy, certified as correct by the authority by whom the application was received, shall not require any legal authentication, and may in any case be deposited at any time within three months from the deposit of the subsequent application. They may require it to be accompanied by a certificate from the proper authority showing the date of the deposit, and also by a translation.

No other formalities may be required for the declaration of priority at the time of depositing the application.

Each of the contracting countries shall decide for itself what consequences shall follow the omission of the formalities prescribed by the present article, but such consequences shall in no case be more serious than the loss of the right of priority.

Subsequently, further proof

(*e*) Lorsqu'un dessin ou modèle industriel aura été déposé dans un pays en vertu d'un droit de priorité basé sur le dépôt d'un modèle d'utilité, le délai de priorité ne sera que celui fixé pour les dessins ou modèles industriels.

En outre, il est permis de déposer dans un pays un modèle d'utilité en vertu d'un droit de priorité basé sur le dépôt d'une demande de brevet et inversement.

(*f*) Si une demande de brevet contient la revendication de priorités multiples, ou si l'examen révèle qu'une demande est complexe, l'Administration devra, tout au moins, autoriser le demandeur à la diviser dans des conditions que déterminera la législation intérieure, en conservant comme date de chaque demande divisionaire la date de la demande initiale et, s'il y a lieu, le bénéfice du droit de priorité.

in support of the declaration may be required.

(*e*) Where an application for the registration of an industrial design or model is deposited in a country in virtue of a right of priority based on a previous deposit of an application for registration of a utility model, the period of priority shall only be that fixed for industrial designs and models.

Further, it is permissible to deposit in a country an application for the registration of a utility model in virtue of a right or priority based on the deposit of a patent application and vice versa.

(*f*) If an application for a patent contains multiple priority claims, or if examination reveals that an application contains more than one invention, the competent authority shall at least authorize the applicant to divide the application, subject to such conditions as may be imposed by domestic legislation, and preserving as the date of each part of the application the date of the initial application and, if necessary, the benefit of the right of priority.

Article 4bis.

Les brevets demandés dans les différents pays contractants par des ressortissants de l'Union seront indépendants des brevets obtenus pour la même invention dans les autres pays, adhérents ou non à l'Union.

Cette disposition doit s'entendre d'une façon absolue, notamment en ce sens que les brevets demandés pendant le

Patents applied for in the various contracting countries by persons entitled to the benefits of the Union shall be independent of the patents obtained for the same invention in the other countries, whether members of the Union or not.

This stipulation must be strictly interpreted, for example, it shall be understood to mean

délai de priorité sont indépendants, tant au point de vue des causes de nullité et de déchéance, qu'au point de vue de la durée normale.

Elle s'applique à tous les brevets existant au moment de sa mise en vigueur.

Il en sera de même, en cas d'accession de nouveaux pays, pour les brevets existant de part et d'autre au moment de l'accession.

that patents applied for during the period of priority are independent, in respect of the grounds for refusal and for revocation, as well as in respect of their normal duration.

The stipulation applies to all patents existing at the time when it comes into effect.

Similarly it shall apply, in the case of the accession of new countries, to patents in existence, either on one side or the other, at the time of accession.

ARTICLE 5.

L'introduction, par le breveté, dans le pays ou le brevet a été délivré, d'objets fabriqués dans l'un ou l'autre des pays de l'Union, n'entraînera pas la déchéance.

Toutefois chacun des pays contractants aura la faculté de prendre les mesures législatives nécessaires pour prévenir les abus qui pourraient résulter de l'exercice du droit exclusif conféré par le brevet, par example faute d'exploitation.

Ces mesures ne pourront prévoir la déchéance du brevet que si la concession de licences obligatoires ne suffisait pas pour prévenir ces abus.

En tout cas, le brevet ne pourra pas faire l'objet de telles mesures avant l'expiration d'au moins trois années à compter de la date où il a été accordé et si le breveté justifie d'excuses légitimes.

La protection des dessins et modèles industriels ne peut être atteinte par une déchéance quelconque pour introduction d'ob-

The importation by the patentee into the country where the patent has been granted of articles manufactured in any of the countries of the Union shall not entail revocation of the patent.

Nevertheless each of the contracting countries shall have the right to take the necessary legislative measures to prevent the abuses which might result from the exercise of the exclusive rights conferred by the patent, for example, failure to work.

These measures shall not provide for the revocation of the patent unless the grant of compulsory licenses is insufficient to prevent such abuses.

In no case can the patent be made liable to such measures before the expiration of at least three years from the date of grant of the patent and then only if the patentee is unable to justify himself by legitimate reasons.

The protection of industrial

jets conformes à ceux qui sont protégés.

Aucun signe ou mention d'enregistrement ne sera exigé sur le produit, pour la reconnaissance du droit.

Si, dans un pays, l'utilisation de la marque enregistrée est obligatoire, l'enregistrement ne pourra être annulé qu'après un délai équitable et si l'interessé ne justifie pas des causes de son inaction.

designs and models may not, under any circumstances, be liable to revocation by reason of the importation of articles corresponding to those which are protected.

No sign or mention of registration shall be required on the goods in order to maintain recognition of the rights given by such registration.

If, in any country, the utilisation of a registered trade mark is compulsory, registration cannot be cancelled until after a reasonable period has elapsed, and then only if the person interested cannot justify the causes of his inaction.

Article 5bis.

Un délai de grâce, qui devra être au minimum de trois mois, sera accordé pour le payement des taxes prévues pour le maintien des droits de propriété industrielle, moyennant le versement d'une surtaxe, si la législation nationale en impose une.

Pour les brevets d'invention, les pays contractants s'engagent en outre, soit à porter le délai de grâce à six mois au moins, soit à prévoir la restauration du brevet tombé en déchéance par suite de non payement de taxes, ces mesures restant soumises aux conditions prévues par la législation intérieure.

An extension of time of not less than three months shall be allowed for the payment of the prescribed fees for the maintenance of industrial property rights, on condition (if the national legislation of a country so provides) of the payment of a supplementary fee.

In the case of patents, the contracting countries further undertake, either to increase the above-mentioned extension of time to not less than six months, or to provide for the restoration of a patent which has expired by reason of the non-payment of fees, subject in each case to the conditions prescribed by the domestic legislation.

Article 5ter.

Dans chacun des pays contractants ne seront pas consi-

In each of the contracting countries the following shall not

dérés comme portant atteinte aux droits du breveté:

1. L'emploi, à bord des navires des autres pays de l'Union, des moyens faisant l'objet de son brevet dans le corps du navire, dans les machines, agrès, apparaux et autres accessoires, lorsque ces navires pénétreront temporairement ou accidentellement dans les eaux du pays, sous réserve que ces moyens y soient employés exclusivement pour les besoins du navire;

2. L'emploi des moyens faisant l'objet du brevet dans la construction ou le fonctionnement des engins de locomotion aérienne ou terrestre des autres pays de l'Union ou des accessoires de ces engins, lorsque ceux-ci pénétreront temporairement ou accidentellement dans ce pays.

be considered as infringements of the rights of a patentee.

1. The use on board vessels of other countries of the Union of a patented invention in the body of the vessel, in the machinery, tackle, apparatus and other accessories, when such vessels penetrate temporarily or accidentally into the territorial waters of the country, provided that such invention is used exclusively for the actual needs of the vessel.

2. The use of a patented invention in the construction or working of aircraft or land vehicles of other countries of the Union, or of the accessories to such aircraft or vehicles, when such aircraft or vehicles penetrate temporarily or accidentally into the country.

ARTICLE 6.

Toute marque de fabrique ou de commerce régulièrement enregistrée dans le pays d'origine sera admise au dépôt et protégée telle quelle dans les autres pays de l'Union.

Toutefois, pourront être refusées ou invalidées:

1. Les marques qui sont de nature à porter atteinte à des droits acquis par des tiers dans le pays où la protection est réclamée.

2. Les marques dépourvues de tout caractère distinctif, ou bien composées exclusivement de signes ou d'indications pouvant servir, dans le commerce, pour désigner l'espèce, la qualité, la quantité, la destination, la valeur, le lieu d'origine des produits ou l'époque de production,

Every trade mark duly registered in the country of origin shall be admitted for deposit and protected in its original form in the other countries of the Union.

Nevertheless, registration of the following may be refused or cancelled:

1. Marks which are of such a nature as to infringe rights acquired by third parties in the country where protection is claimed.

2. Marks which have no distinctive character, or which consist exclusively of signs or indications which serve in trade to designate the kind, quality, quantity, destination, value, place of origin of the goods or date of production, or which

ou devenus usuels dans le langage courant ou les habitudes loyales et constantes du commerce du pays où la protection est réclamée.

Dans l'appréciation du caractère distinctif d'une marque on devra tenir compte de toutes les circonstances de fait, notamment de la durée de l'usage de la marque.

3. Les marques qui sont contraires à la morale ou à l'ordre public.

Il est entendu qu'une marque ne pourra être considérée comme contraire à l'ordre public pour la seule raison qu'elle n'est pas conforme à quelque disposition de la législation sur les marques, sauf le cas où cette disposition elle-même concerne l'ordre public.

Sera considéré comme pays d'origine:

Le pays de l'Union où le déposant a un établissement industriel ou commercial effectif et sérieux, et, s'il n'a pas un tel établissement, le pays de l'Union où il a son domicile et, s'il n'a pas de domicile dans l'Union, le pays de sa nationalité au cas ou il est ressortissant d'un pays de l'Union.

En aucun cas le renouvellement de l'enregistrement d'une marque dans le pays d'origine n'entraînera l'obligation de renouveler l'enregistrement dans les autres pays de l'Union où la marque aura été enregistrée.

Le bénéfice de la priorité reste acquis aux dépôts de marques effectués dans le délai de l'article 4, même lorsque l'enregistrement dans le pays d'origine

have become customary in the current language, or in the bona fide and recognised customs of the trade of the country where protection is claimed.

In arriving at a decision as to the distinctive character of a mark, all the circumstances of the case must be taken into account, including the length of time during which the mark has been in use.

3. Marks which are contrary to morality or public order.

It is understood that a mark cannot be considered as contrary to public order for the sole reason that it does not conform to some stipulation of the laws concerning marks, except where such stipulation itself relates to public order.

Shall be considered as the country of origin:

The country of the Union where the depositor has a real and effective industrial or commercial establishment; if he has not such an establishment, the country of the Union where he is domiciled, and if he is not domiciled in the Union the country of his nationality if he is a person within the jurisdiction of one of the countries of the Union.

In no case shall the renewal of the registration of a mark in the country of origin involve the obligation to renew the registration of the mark in other countries of the Union where it has been registered.

The benefits of priority shall be accorded to applications for the registration of marks deposited within the period fixed

n'intervient qu'après l'expiration de ce délai.

La disposition de l'alinéa 1 n'exclut pas le droit d'exiger du déposant un certificat d'enregistrement régulier, délivré par l'autorité compétente du pays d'origine, mais aucune légalisation ne sera requise pour ce certificat.

by Article 4, notwithstanding the fact that registration in the country of origin, may not be completed until after the expiration of such period.

The stipulations of paragraph 1 do not exclude the right of requiring from a depositor a certificate of due registration, issued by the competent authority of the country of origin, but no legal authentication of such certificate shall be required.

Article 6bis.

Les pays contractants s'engagent à refuser ou à invalider soit d'office si la législation du pays le permet, soit à la requête de l'intéressé, l'enregistrement d'une marque de fabrique ou de commerce qui serait la reproduction ou l'imitation susceptible de faire confusion, d'une marque que l'autorité compétente du pays de l'enregistrement estimera y être notoirement connue comme étant déjà la marque d'un ressortissant d'un autre pays contractant et utilisée pour des produits du même genre ou d'un genre similaire.

Un délai minimum de 3 ans devra être accordé pour réclamer la radiation de ces marques. Le délai courra de la date de l'enregistrement de la marque.

Il ne sera pas fixé de délai pour réclamer la radiation des marques enregistrés de mauvaise foi.

The contracting countries undertake to refuse or to cancel, either administratively if their legislation so permits, or at the request of an interested party, the registration of any trade mark which is a reproduction of or an imitation capable of creating confusion with a mark considered by the competent authority of the country of registration to be well-known in that country as being already the mark of a person within the jurisdiction of another contracting country, and utilised for the same or similar classes of goods.

A period of at least three years shall be allowed for claiming the removal of such marks. This period shall run from the date of registration of the mark.

There shall be no limit to the period within which application may be made for the removal of marks registered in bad faith.

Article 6ter.

Les pays contractants conviennent de refuser ou d'in-

The contracting countries agree to refuse or to cancel the

valider l'enregistrement et d'interdire, par des mesures appropriées, l'utilisation, à défaut d'autorisation des pouvoirs compétents, soit comme marques de fabrique ou de commerce, soit comme éléments de ces marques, des armoiries, drapeaux et autres emblêmes d'Etat des pays contractants, signes et poinçons officiels de contrôle et de garantie adoptés par eux, ainsi que toute imitation au point de vue héraldique.

L'interdiction des signes et poinçons officiels de contrôle et de garantie s'appliquera seulement dans les cas où les marques qui les comprendront seront destinées à être útilisées sur des marchandises du même genre ou d'un genre similaire.

Pour l'application de ces dispositions les pays contractants conviennent de se communiquer réciproquement, par l'intermédiaire du Bureau international de Berne, la liste des emblêmes d'Etat, signes et poinçons officiels de contrôle et de garantie, qu'ils désirent ou désireront placer, d'une façon absolue ou dans certaines limites, sous la protection du présent article, ainsi que toutes modifications ultérieures apportées à cette liste. Chaque pays contractant mettra à la disposition du public, en temps utile, les listes notifiées.

Tout pays contractant pourra, dans un délai de douze mois à partir de la reception de la notification, transmettre, par l'intermédiaire du Bureau international de Berne, au pays intéressé, ses objections éventuelles.

registration, and to prohibit by appropriate measures the utilisation, without authorisation by the competent authorities, either as trade marks or as elements of trade marks, of armorial bearings, flags and other State emblems of the contracting countries, official signs and hall-marks indicating control or warranty adopted by them, and all imitations thereof from an heraldic point of view.

The prohibition of the utilisation of official signs and hall-marks indicating control or warranty shall apply solely in cases where the marks which contain them are intended to be utilised for the same or similar classes of goods.

For the application of these stipulations the contracting countries agree to communicate mutually through the medium of the International Bureau of Berne, the list of State emblems and official signs and hall-marks indicating control or warranty which they desire, or may hereafter desire, to place wholly or within certain limits, under the protection of the present Article, and all subsequent modifications of this list. Each contracting country shall forthwith make the lists so communicated available to the public.

Any contracting country may, within a period of twelve months from the receipt of the communication, transmit any objections which it may desire to offer to the country concerned through the medium of the International Bureau.

In the case of State emblems which are well-known the meas-

Pour les emblêmes d'Etat notoirement connus, les mesures prévues à l'alinéa 1 s'appliqueront seulement aux marques enregistrées après la signature du présent Acte.

Pour les emblêmes d'État qui ne seraient pas notoirement connus, et pour les signes et poinçons officiels, ces dispositions ne seront applicables qu'aux marques enregistrées plus de deux mois après reception de la notification prévue par l'alinéa 3.

En cas de mauvaise foi, les pays auront la faculté de radier même les marques enregistrées avant la signature du présent Acte et comportant des emblêmes d'Etat, signes et poinçons.

Les nationaux de chaque pays qui seraient autorisés à faire usage des emblêmes d'Etat, signes et poinçons de leur pays, pourront les utiliser, même s'il y avait similitude avec ceux d'un autre pays.

Les pays contractants s'engagent à interdire l'usage non autorisé, dans le commerce, des armoiries d'États des autres pays contractants, lorsque cet usage sera de nature à induire en erreur sur l'origine des produits.

Les dispositions qui précèdent ne font pas obstacle à l'exercice, par les pays, de la faculté de refuser ou d'invalider, par application du No. 3 de l'alinéa 2 de l'article 6, les marques contenant, sans autorisation, des armoiries, drapeaux, décorations et autres emblêmes d'État ou des signes et poinçons officiels adoptés par un pays de l'Union.

ures prescribed by paragraph 1 shall apply solely to marks registered after the signature of the present Convention.

As regards State emblems which are not well-known and official signs and hall-marks, such stipulations shall be applicable only to marks registered more than two months after the receipt of the communication provided for in paragraph 3.

In cases of bad faith, however, each country shall be entitled to cause removal of marks, even though registered before the signature of the present Convention if they contain State emblems, signs or hall-marks.

The nationals of each country who have been authorised to make use of State emblems, signs or hall-marks of their country, may continue to use them even though they are similar to those of another country.

The contracting countries undertake to prohibit the unauthorised use in trade of the State armorial bearings of the other contracting countries, when such use is of a nature to cause deception as to the origin of the goods.

The above stipulations shall not prevent the countries from exercising the power given in the third subsection of paragraph 2 of Article 6, to refuse or to cancel the registration of marks containing, without authorisation, the armorial bearings, flags, decorations, and other State emblems or official signs or hall-marks adopted by a country of the Union.

ARTICLE 7.

La nature du produit sur lequel la marque de fabrique ou de commerce doit être apposée ne peut, dans aucun cas, faire obstacle à l'enregistrement de la marque.

The nature of the goods to which the trade mark is to be applied can, in no case, form an obstacle to the registration of the mark.

ARTICLE 7bis.

Les pays contractants s'engagent à admettre au dépôt et à protéger les marques appartenant à des collectivités dont l'existence n'est pas contraire à la loi du pays d'origine, même si ces collectivités ne possèdent pas un établissement industriel ou commercial.

Cependant chaque pays sera juge des conditions particulières sous lesquelles une collectivité pourra être admise à faire protéger ses marques.

The contracting countries undertake to admit to deposit and to protect marks belonging to associations, the existence of which is not contrary to the law of the country of origin, even if such associations do not possess an industrial or commercial establishment.

Nevertheless, each country shall be the sole judge of the particular conditions under which an association may be allowed to obtain protection for its marks.

ARTICLE 8.

Le nom commercial sera protégé dans tous les pays de l'Union sans obligation de dépôt ou d'enregistrement, qu'il fasse ou non partie d'une marque de fabrique ou de commerce.

A trade name shall be protected in all the countries of the Union without necessity of deposit or registration, whether or not it forms part of a trade mark.

ARTICLE 8bis.

Tout produit portant illicitement une marque de fabrique ou de commerce, ou un non commercial, sera saisi à l'importation dans ceux des pays de l'Union dans lesquels cette marque ou ce nom commercial ont droit à la protection légale.

La saisie sera également effectuée dans le pays ou l'ap-

All goods illegally bearing a trade mark or trade name shall be seized on importation into those countries of the Union where this mark or name has a right to legal protection.

Seizure shall be effected equally in the country where the mark or name was illegally applied, or in the country into

position illicite aura eu lieu, ou dans le pays ou aura été importé le produit.

La saisie aura lieu à la requête soit du ministère public, soit de toute autre autorité compétente, soit d'une partie intéressée, personne physique ou morale, conformément à la législation intérieure de chaque pays.

Les autorités ne seront pas tenues d'effectuer la saisie en cas de transit.

Si la législation d'un pays n'admet pas la saisie à l'importation, la saisie sera remplacée par la prohibition d'importation ou la saisie à l'intérieur.

Si la législation d'un pays n'admet ni la saisie à l'importation, ni la prohibition d'importation, ni la saisie à l'intérieur, et en attendant que cette législation soit modifiée en conséquence, ces mesures seront remplacées par les actions et moyens que la loi de ce pays assurerait en pareil cas aux nationaux.

which the goods bearing it may have been imported.

The seizure shall take place at the request either of the Public Prosecutor or of any other competent authority or of any interested party whether an individual or a body of persons corporate or unincorporate in conformity with the domestic law of each country.

The authorities shall not be bound to effect the seizure of goods in transit.

If the laws of a country do not admit of seizure on importation, such seizure shall be replaced by prohibition of importation or seizure within such country.

If the laws of any country do not admit of seizure on importation, or of prohibition of importation, or of seizure within the country, and pending the requisite modification of these laws, these measures shall be replaced by the remedies available in such cases to nationals.

Article 10.

Les dispositions de l'article précédent seront applicables à tout produit portant faussement, comme indication de provenance, le nom d'une localité ou d'un pays déterminé, lorsque cette indication sera jointe à un nom commercial fictif ou emprunté dans une intention frauduleuse.

Sera en tous cas reconnu comme partie intéressé, que ce soit une personne physique ou morale, tout producteur, fabricant ou commercant engagé dans la production, la fabrica-

The stipulations of the preceding article shall be applicable to all goods which falsely bear as an indication of origin the name of a specified locality or country, when such indication is joined to a trade name of a fictitious character or used with fraudulent intention.

Any producer, manufacturer or trader, whether an individual or a body of persons corporate or incorporate, engaged in the production, manufacture, or trade of such goods, and established either in the

tion ou le commerce de ce produit et établi soit dans la localité faussement indiquée comme lieu de provenance, soit dans la région où cette localité est située, soit dans le pays faussement indiqué.

locality falsely indicated as the place of origin, in the district where the locality is situated, or in the country falsely indicated shall in any case be deemed a party interested.

ARTICLE 10bis.

Les pays contractants sont tenus d'assurer aux ressortissants de l'Union une protection effective contre la concurrence déloyale.

Constitue un acte de concurrence déloyale tout acte de concurrence contraire aux usages honnêtes en matière industrielle ou commerciale.

Notamment devront être interdits:

1. tous faits quelconques de nature à créer une confusion par n'importe quel moyen avec les produits d'un concurrent;

2. les allégations fausses, dans l'exercice du commerce, de nature à discréditer les produits d'un concurrent.

The contracting countries are bound to assure to persons entitled to the benefits of the Union an effective protection against unfair competition.

Every act of competition contrary to honest practices in industrial or commercial matters constitutes an act of unfair competition.

The following acts among others shall be prohibited:

1. All manner of acts, of such a nature as to create confusion by any means whatsoever with the goods of a competitor;

2. False allegations, in the course of trade, of such a nature as to discredit the goods of a competitor.

ARTICLE 10ter.

Les pays contractants s'engagent à assurer aux ressortissants des autres pays de l'Union des recours légaux appropriés pour réprimer efficacement tous les actes visés aux articles 9, 10 et 10bis.

Ils s'engagent, en outre, à prévoir des mesures pour permettre aux syndicats et associations représentant l'industrie ou le commerce intéressé et dont l'existence n'est pas contraire aux lois de leur pays, d'agir en justice ou auprès des autorités administratives, en vue de la

The contracting countries undertake to assure to persons within the jurisdiction of other countries of the Union appropriate legal remedies to repress effectively all acts referred to in Articles 9, 10 and 10bis.

They undertake, further, to provide measures to permit syndicates and associations which represent industries or trades interested, and of which the existence is not contrary to the laws of their country, to take proceedings in the Courts or before the administrative

répression des actes prévus par les articles 9, 10 et 10bis, dans la mesure où la loi du pays dans lequel la protection est réclamée le permet aux syndicats et associations de ce pays.

authorities with a view to securing repression of the acts referred to in Articles 9, 10 and 10bis so far as the law of the country in which protection is claimed permits such action to the syndicates and associations of that country.

ARTICLE 11.

Les pays contractants accorderont, conformément à leur législation intérieure, une protection temporaire aux inventions brevetables, aux modèles d'utilité, aux dessins ou modèles industriels ainsi qu'aux marques de fabrique ou de commerce, pour les produits qui figureront aux expositions internationales officielles ou officiellement reconnues, organisées sur le territoire de l'un d'eux.

Cette protection temporaire ne prolongera pas les délais de l'article 4. Si plus tard le droit de priorité est invoqué, l'Administration de chaque pays pourra faire partir le délai de la date de l'introduction du produit dans l'exposition.

Chaque pays pourra exiger, comme preuve de l'identité de l'objet exposé et de la date d'introduction, les pièces justificatives qu'il jugera nécessaires.

The contracting countries shall, in conformity with their domestic legislation, grant temporary protection to patentable inventions, utility models, industrial designs or models, and trade marks, in respect of goods exhibited at official, or officially recognised, international exhibitions held in the territory of one of them.

This temporary protection shall not prolong the periods of priority provided by Article 4. If, at a later date, the right of priority is invoked, the Administration of each country may date the period of priority as from the date of introduction of the goods into the exhibition.

Each country may require, as proof of the identity of the object exhibited, and of the date of its introduction into the exhibition such evidence as it may consider necessary.

ARTICLE 12.

Chacun des pays contractants s'engage à établir un service spécial de la propriété industrielle et un dépôt central pour la communication au public des brevets d'invention, des modèles d'utilité, des dessins ou modèles industriels et des

Each of the contracting countries undertakes to establish a special Government department for industrial property, and a central office for communication to the public of patents, utility models, industrial designs or models, and trade marks.

marques de fabrique ou de commerce.

Ce service publiera une feuille périodique officielle.

This department shall publish an official periodical journal.

ARTICLE 13.

L'Office international institué à Berne sous le nom de Bureau international pour la protection de la propriété industrielle est placé sous la haute autorité du Gouvernement de la Confédération suisse, qui en règle l'organisation et en surveille le fonctionnement.

La langue officielle du Bureau international est la langue française.

Le Bureau international centralise les renseignements de toute nature relatifs à la protection de la propriété industrielle, il les réunit et les publie. Il procède aux études d'utilité commune intéressant l'Union et rédige, à l'aide des documents qui sont mis à sa disposition par les diverses Administrations, une feuille périodique, en langue française, sur les questions concernant l'objet de l'Union.

Les numéros de cette feuille, de même que tous les documents publiés par le Bureau international, sont répartis entre les Administrations des pays de l'Union dans la proportion du nombre des unités contributives ci-dessous mentionnées. Les exemplaires et documents supplémentaires qui seraient réclamés, soit par lesdites Administrations, soit par des societés ou des particuliers, seront payés à part.

Le Bureau international doit se tenir en tout temps à la disposition des pays de l'Union,

The International Office, established at Berne under the name "Bureau international pour la Protection de la Propriété Industrielle" is placed under the high authority of the Government of the Swiss Confederation, which regulates its organisation and supervises its working.

The official language of the International Bureau is French.

The International Bureau centralises information of every kind relating to the protection of industrial property and collates and publishes it. It studies matters of general utility which interest the Union, and edits, with the help of documents supplied to it by the various Administrations, a periodical journal in French, dealing with questions concerning the object of the Union.

The numbers of this journal, as well as all the documents published by the International Bureau, are circulated among the Administrations of the countries of the Union in the proportion of the number of contributing units as mentioned below. Such further copies as may be desired, either by the said Administrations, or by societies or private persons shall be paid for separately.

The International Bureau shall at all times hold itself at the service of countries of the Union, in order to supply them

pour leur fournir, sur les questions relatives au service international de la propriété industrielle, les renseignements spéciaux dont ils pourraient avoir besoin. Le Directeur du Bureau international fait sur sa gestion un rapport annuel qui est communiqué à tous les pays de l'Union.

Les dépenses du Bureau international seront supportées en commun par les pays contractants. Jusqu'à nouvel ordre, elles ne pourront pas dépasser la somme de cent vingt mille francs suisses par année. Cette somme pourra être augmentée, au besoin, par décision unanime d'une des Conférences prévues à l'article 14.

Pour déterminer la part contributive de chacun des pays dans cette somme totale des frais, les pays contractants et ceux qui adhéront ultérieurement à l'Union sont divisés en six classes contribuant chacune dans la proportion d'un certain nombre d'unités, savoir:

1re	classe	25	unités
2e	"	20	"
3e	"	15	"
4e	"	10	"
5e	"	5	"
6e	"	3	"

Ces coefficients sont multipliés par le nombre des pays de chaque classe, et la somme des produits obtenus fournit le nombre d'unités par lequel la dépense totale doit être divisée. Le quotient donne le montant de l'unité de dépense.

Chacun des pays contractants désignera, au moment de

with any special information they may need on questions relating to the international system of industrial property. The Director of the International Bureau will furnish an annual report on its working, which shall be communicated to all the countries of the Union.

The expenses of the International Bureau shall be borne by the contracting countries in common. Until fresh sanction is given, they must not exceed the sum of 120,000 Swiss francs per annum. This sum may be increased, in case of necessity, by a unanimous decision of one of the conferences referred to in Article 14.

To determine the quota which each country should contribute to this common total of expenses, the contracting countries and those which may afterwards join the Union are divided into six classes, each contributing in the proportion of a certain number of units, namely:

1st	class	25	units
2nd	"	20	"
3rd	"	15	"
4th	"	10	"
5th	"	5	"
6th	"	3	"

These co-efficients are multiplied by the number of countries in each class, and the sum of the products thus obtained gives the number of units by which the total expense has to be divided. The quotient gives the amount of the unit of expense.

son accession, la classe dans laquelle il désire être rangé.

Le Gouvernement de la Confédération suisse surveille les dépenses du Bureau international, fait les avances nécessaires et établit le compte annuel qui sera communiqué à toutes les autres Administrations.

Each of the contracting countries will designate at the time of its accession the class in which it wishes to be placed.

The Government of the Swiss Confederation superintends the expenses of the International Bureau, advances the necessary funds and renders an annual account, which will be communicated to all the other Administrations.

ARTICLE 14.

La présente Convention sera soumise à des révisions périodiques, en vue d'y introduire les améliorations de nature à perfectionner le système de l'Union.

A cet effet, des Conférences auront lieu, successivement, dans l'un des pays contractants entre les Délégués desdits pays.

L'Administration du pays ou doit siéger la Conférence préparara, avec le concours du Bureau international, les travaux de cette Conférence.

Le Directeur du Bureau international assistera aux séances des Conférences, et prendra part aux discussions sans voix délibérative.

The present Convention shall be submitted to periodical revisions with a view to the introduction of amendments calculated to improve the system of the Union.

For this purpose, Conferences shall be held, successively in one of the contracting countries, among the delegates of the said countries.

The Administration of the country in which the Conference is to be held will make preparations for the work of that Conference, with the assistance of the International Bureau.

The Director of the International Bureau will be present at the meetings of the Conferences and will take part in the discussions, but without the right of voting.

ARTICLE 15.

Il est entendu que les pays contractants se réservent respectivement le droit de prendre séparément, entre eux, des arrangements particuliers pour la protection de la propriété industrielle, en tant que ces arrangements ne contreviendraient

It is understood that the contracting countries respectively reserve to themselves the right to make separately, as between themselves, special arrangements for the protection of industrial property, in so far as such agreements do not contrapoint aux dispositions de la présente Convention.

vene the stipulations of the present Convention.

ARTICLE 16.

Les pays qui n'ont point pris part à la présente Convention seront admis à y adhérer sur leur demande.

Cette adhésion sera notifié par la voie diplomatique au Gouvernement de la Confédération suisse et par celui-ci à tous les autres.

Elle emportera, de plein droit, accession à toutes les clauses et admission à tous les avantages stipulés par la présente Convention, et produira ses effets un mois après l'envoi de la notification faite par le Gouvernement de la Confédération suisse aux autres pays unionistes, à moins qu'une date postérieure n'ait été indiquée par le pays adhérent.

Countries which are not parties to the present Convention shall be allowed to accede to it upon their request.

This accession shall be notified through diplomatic channels to the Government of the Swiss Confederation, and by the latter to all the other countries.

It shall entail, as a matter of right, accession to all the clauses, and admission to all the advantages stipulated in the present Convention, and shall take effect one month after the dispatch of the notification by the Government of the Swiss Confederation to the other countries of the Union, unless a subsequent date has been indicated by the acceding country.

ARTICLE 16bis.

Les pays contractants ont le droit d'accéder en tout temps à la présente Convention pour leurs colonies, possessions, dépendances et protectorats, ou territoires administrés en vertu d'un mandat de la Société des Nations, ou pour certains d'entre eux.

Ils peuvent à cet effet soit faire une déclaration générale par laquelle toutes leurs colonies, possessions, dépendances et protectorats et les territoires visés à l'alinéa 1, sont compris dans l'accession, soit nommer expressément ceux qui y sont compris, soit se borner à indiquer ceux qui en sont exclus.

The contracting countries have the right of acceding to the present Convention at any time, on behalf of their Colonies, Possessions, Dependencies and Protectorates, or territories administered in virtue of a mandate from the League of Nations, or of any of them.

For this purpose they may either make a general declaration, including all their Colonies, Possessions, Dependencies and Protectorates, and the territories referred to in paragraph 1, in the accession, or may expressly name those which are included, or may confine them-

Cette déclaration sera notifiée par écrit au Gouvernement de la Confédération suisse et par celui-ci à tous les autres.

Les pays contractants pourront, dans les mêmes conditions, dénoncer la Convention pour leurs colonies, possessions, dépendances et protectorats, ou pour les territoires visés à l'alinéa 1, ou pour certains d'entre eux.

selves to indicating those which are excluded therefrom.

This declaration shall be notified in writing to the Government of the Swiss Confederation and by the latter to all the other countries.

Under the same conditions, the contracting countries may denounce the Convention on behalf of their Colonies, Possessions, Dependencies, and Protectorates, or the territories referred to in paragraph 1, or of any of them.

ARTICLE 17.

L'exécution des engagements réciproques contenus dans la présente Convention est subordonnée, en tant que le besoin, à l'accomplissement des formalités et règles établies par les lois constitutionnelles de ceux des pays contractants qui sont tenus d'en provoquer l'application, ce qu'ils s'obligent à faire dans le plus bref délai possible.

The carrying out of the reciprocal engagements contained in the present Convention is subject, so far as necessary, to the observance of the formalities and rules established by the constitutional laws of those of the contracting countries which are bound to procure their application which they engage to do with as little delay as possible.

ARTICLE 17bis.

La Convention demeurera en vigueur pendant un temps indéterminé, jusqu'à l'expiration d'une année à partir du jour où la dénonciation en sera faite.

Cette dénonciation sera adressée au Gouvernement de la Confédération suisse. Elle ne produira son effet qu'a l'égard du pays qui l'aura faite, la Convention restant exécutoire pour les autres pays contractants.

The Convention shall remain in force for an unlimited time, till the expiry of one year from the date of its denunciation.

This denunciation shall be addressed to the Government of the Swiss Confederation. It shall only affect the denouncing country, the Convention remaining in operation as regards the other contracting countries.

ARTICLE 18.

Le présent Acte sera ratifié et les ratifications en seront dé-

The present Act shall be ratified and the ratifications

posées à La Haye au plus tard le 1er mai 1928. Il entrera en vigueur, entre les pays qui l'auront ratifié, un mois après cette date. Toutefois si auparavant il était ratifié par six pays au moins, il entrerait en vigueur, entre ces pays, un mois après que le dépôt de la sixième ratification leur aurait été notifié par le Gouvernement de la Confédération suisse et, pour les pays qui ratifieraient ensuite, un mois après la notification de chacune de ces ratifications.

Cet Acte remplacera, dans les rapports entre les pays qui l'auront ratifié, la Convention d'Union de Paris de 1883 revisée à Washington le 2 juin 1911 et le Protocole de clôture, lesquels resteront en vigueur dans les rapports avec les pays qui n'auront pas ratifié le présent Acte.

deposited at The Hague not later than the 1st May, 1928. It shall come into force, between the countries which shall have ratified it, one month after that date. Nevertheless, if before that date it has been ratified by at least six countries, it shall come into force, between those countries, one month after the deposit of the sixth ratification has been notified to them by the Government of the Swiss Confederation and, in the case of countries which may ratify at a later date, one month after the notification of each of such ratifications.

This Act shall, as regards the relations between the countries which ratify it, replace the Convention of Paris of 1883, revised at Washington on the 2nd June, 1911, and the Final Protocol, which shall, however, remain in force as regards relations with the countries which shall not have ratified the present Act.

ARTICLE 19.

Le présent Acte sera signé en un seul exemplaire, lequel sera déposé aux archives du Gouvernement des Pays-Bas. Une copie certifiée sera remise par ce dernier à chacun des Gouvernements des pays contractants.

En foi de quoi les Plénipotentiaires respectifs ont signé le présent Acte.

Fait à La Haye, en un seul exemplaire, le 6 novembre, 1925.

The present Act shall be signed in a single copy, which shall be deposited in the archives of the Government of the Netherlands. A certified copy shall be forwarded by the latter to each of the Governments of the contracting countries.

In witness whereof the respective Plenipotentiaries have signed the present Act.

Done at The Hague, in a single copy, the 6th November, 1925.

The member countries of the Industrial Property Union are the following:

Australia
Austria
Belgium
Brazil
Bulgaria
Canada
Cuba
Czechoslovakia
Denmark (including Feroe Islands)
Danzig
Dominican Republic
Esthonia
Finland
France (including Algeria and Colonies)
Germany
Great Britain (including Ceylon, New Zealand and Trinidad and Tobago)
Greece
Hungary
Irish Free State
Italy
Japan
Latvia
Luxemburg
Morocco (French Zone)
Mexico
The Netherlands (including Dutch Indies, Surinam and Curaçao)
Norway
Poland
Portugal (including the Azores and Madeira)
Rumania
Serb-Croat-Slovene State
Spain
Sweden
Switzerland
Syria and Lebanon
Tunis
Turkey, and
The United States of America

The amended Convention as revised at the Conference of The Hague, November 6, 1925, was ratified by:

Austria
Canada
Germany
Great Britain and the Northern Islands
Italy
The Netherlands
Portugal, and
Serb-Croat-Slovene State

IV.

Madrid Arrangement for International Registration of Trade Marks.[1]

(Signed at The Hague, November 6, 1925.)

Article 1.

Les ressortissants de chacun des pays contractants pourront s'assurer, dans tous les autres pays, la protection de leurs marques de fabrique ou de commerce enregistrées dans le pays d'origine, moyennant le dépôt desdites marques au Bureau international, à Berne, fait par l'entremise de l'Administration dudit pays d'origine.

Fait règle pour la définition du pays d'origine, la disposition y relative de l'article 6 de la Convention générale d'Union pour la protection de la propriété industrielle.

Article 2.

Sont assimilés aux ressortissants des pays contractants les sujets ou citoyens des pays n'ayant pas adhéré au présent Arrangement qui, sur le territoire de l'Union restreinte constituée par ce dernier, satisfont aux conditions établies par l'article 3 de la Convention générale.

Article 3.

Toute demande d'enregistrement international devra être présentée sur le formulaire prescrit par le Règlement d'exécution, et l'Administration du pays d'origine de la marque certifiera que les indications qui figurent sur ces demandes correspondent à celles du registre national.

Si le déposant revendique la couleur à titre d'élément distinctif de sa marque, il sera tenu:

1. De le déclarer et d'accompagner son dépôt d'une mention indiquant la couleur ou la combinaison de couleurs revendiquée;

2. De joindre à sa demande des exemplaires de ladite marque en couleur, qui seront annexés aux notifications faites par le Bureau international. Le nombre de ces exemplaires sera fixé par le Règlement d'exécution.

Le Bureau international enregistrera immédiatement les marques déposées conformément à l'article premier. Il notifiera cet enregistremant sans retard aux diverses Administrations. Les marques enregistrées seront publiées dans une feuille périodique éditée par le Bureau international, au moyen des indications contenues dans la demande d'enregistrement et d'un cliché fourni par le déposant.

[1] The text taken is from *Actes de la Conférence de La Haye de l'Union pour la Protection de la Propriété Industrielle*, Berne, 1926, p. 619.

En vue de la publicité à donner, dans les pays contractants, aux marques enregistrées, chaque Administration recevra gratuitement du Bureau international le nombre d'exemplaires de la susdite publication qu'il lui plaira de demander. Cette publicité sera considérée dans tous les pays contractants comme pleinement suffisante, et aucune autre ne pourra être exigée du déposant.

Article 4.

A partir de l'enregistrement ainsi fait au Bureau international, la protection de la marque dans chacun des pays contractants sera la même que si cette marque y avait été directement déposée.

Toute marque qui a été l'objet d'un enregistrement international jouira du droit de priorité établi par l'article 4 de la Convention générale, sans qu'il soit nécessaire d'accomplir les formalités prévues dans la lettre *d* de cet article.

Article 4bis.

Lorsqu'une marque, déjà déposée dans un ou plusieurs des pays contractants, a été postérieurement enregistrée par le Bureau international au nom du même titulaire ou de son ayant cause, l'enregistrement international sera considéré comme substitué aux enregistrements nationaux antérieurs, sans préjudice des droits acquis par le fait de ces derniers.

Article 5.

Dans les pays où leur législation les y autorise, les Administrations auxquelles le Bureau international notifiera l'enregistrement d'une marque, auront la faculté de déclarer que la protection ne peut être accordée à cette marque sur leur territoire. Un tel refus ne pourra être opposé que dans les conditions qui s'appliqueraient, en vertu de la Convention générale, à une marque déposée à l'enregistrement national.

Les Administrations qui voudront exercer cette faculté devront notifier leurs refus, avec indication des motifs, au Bureau international dans le délai prévu par leur loi nationale, et, au plus tard, avant la fin d'une année comptée à partir de l'enregistrement international de la marque.

Le Bureau international transmettra sans retard à l'Administration du pays d'origine et au propriétaire de la marque ou à son mandataire, si celui-ci a été indiqué au Bureau par ladite Administration, un des exemplaires de la déclaration de refus ainsi notifiée. L'intéressé aura les mêmes moyens de recours que si la marque avait été par lui directement déposée dans le pays où la protection est refusée.

Les Administrations qui, dans le délai maximum susindiqué d'un an, n'auront adressé aucune communication au Bureau international seront censées avoir accepté la marque.

ARTICLE 5bis.

Les pièces justificatives de la légitimité d'usage de certains éléments contenus dans les marques, tels que armoiries, écussons, portraits, distinctions honorifiques, titres, noms commerciaux ou noms de personnes autres que celui du déposant, ou autres inscriptions analogues, qui pourraient être réclamées par les Administrations des pays contractants, seront dispensées de toute certification ou légalisation autre que celle de l'Administration du pays d'origine.

ARTICLE 5ter.

Le Bureau international délivrera à toute personne qui en fera la demande, moyennant une taxe fixée par le Règlement d'exécution, une copie des mentions inscrites dans le Registre relativement à une marque déterminée.

Il pourra aussi, contre rémunération, se charger de faire des recherches d'antériorité parmi les marques internationales.

ARTICLE 6.

La protection résultant de l'enregistrement au Bureau international durera vingt ans à partir de cet enregistrement (sous réserve de ce qui est prévu à l'article 8 pour le cas où le déposant n'aura versé qu'une fraction de l'émolument international), mais elle ne pourra être invoquée en faveur d'une marque qui ne jouirait plus de la protection légale dans le pays d'origine.

ARTICLE 7.

L'enregistrement pourra toujours être renouvelé suivant les prescriptions des articles 1 et 3 pour une nouvelle période de vingt ans à compter depuis la date de renouvellement.

Six mois avant l'expiration du terme de protection, le Bureau international rappellera au propriétaire de la marque, par l'envoi d'un avis officieux, la date exacte de cette expiration.

Si la marque présentée en renouvellement du précédent dépôt a subi une modification de forme, les Administrations pourront se refuser à l'enregistrer à titre de renouvellement et le même droit leur appartiendra en cas de changement dans l'indication des produits auxquels la marque doit s'appliquer, à moins que, sur notification de l'objection par l'intermédiaire du Bureau international, l'intéressé ne déclare renoncer à la protection pour les produits autres que ceux désignés en mêmes termes lors de l'enregistrement antérieur.

Lorsque la marque n'est pas admise à titre de renouvellement, il pourra être tenu compte des droits d'antériorité ou autres acquis par le fait de l'enregistrement antérieur.

Article 8.

L'Administration du pays d'origine fixera à son gré, et percevra à son profit, une taxe nationale qu'elle réclamera du propriétaire de la marque dont l'enregistrement international est demandé.

A cette taxe s'ajoutera un émolument international (en francs suisses) de cent cinquante francs pour la première marque, et de cent francs pour chacune des marques suivantes, déposées en même temps au Bureau international au nom du même propriétaire.

Le déposant aura la faculté de n'acquitter au moment du dépôt international qu'un émolument de cent francs pour la première marque et de soixante-quinze francs pour chacune des marques déposées en même temps que la première.

Si le déposant fait usage de cette faculté, il devra, avant l'expiration d'un délai de dix ans compté à partir de l'enregistrement international, verser au Bureau international un complément d'émolument de soixante-quinze francs pour la première marque et de cinquante francs pour chacune des marques déposées en même temps que la première, faute de quoi, à l'expiration de ce délai, il perdra le bénéfice de son enregistrement. Six mois avant cette expiration, le Bureau international rappellera au déposant, par l'envoi d'un avis officieux, à toutes fins utiles, la date exacte de cette expiration. Si le complément d'émolument n'est pas versé avant l'expiration de ce délai au Bureau international, celui-ci radiera la marque, notifiera cette opération aux Administrations et la publiera dans son journal.

Lorsque la liste des produits pour lesquels la protection est revendiquée contiendra plus de cent mots, l'enregistrement de la marque ne sera effectué qu'après payement d'une surtaxe à fixer par le Règlement d'exécution.

Le produit annuel des diverses recettes de l'enregistrement international sera réparti par parts égales entre les pays contractants par les soins du Bureau international, après déduction des frais communs nécessités par l'exécution du présent Arrangement.

Si, au moment de l'entrée en vigueur du présent Arrangement revisé, un pays ne l'a pas encore ratifié, il n'aura droit, jusqu'à la date de son adhésion postérieure, qu'à une répartition de l'excédent de recettes calculé sur la base des anciennes taxes.

Article 8bis.

Le propriétaire d'une marque internationale peut toujours renoncer à la protection dans un ou plusieurs des pays contractants, au moyen d'une déclaration remise à l'Administration du pays d'origine de la marque, pour être communiquée au Bureau international, qui la notifiera aux pays que cette renonciation concerne.

Article 9.

L'Administration du pays d'origine notifiera au Bureau international les annulations, radiations, renonciations, transmissions et autres changements apportés à l'inscription de la marque.

Le Bureau inscrira ces changements dans le Registre international, les notifiera à son tour aux Administrations des pays contractants, et les publiera dans son journal.

On procédera de même lorsque le propriétaire de la marque demandera à réduire la liste des produits auxquels elle s'applique.

Ces opérations peuvent être soumises à une taxe qui sera fixée par le Règlement d'exécution.

L'addition ultérieure d'un nouveau produit à la liste ne peut être obtenue que par un nouveau dépôt effectué conformément aux prescriptions de l'article 3.

A l'addition est assimilée la substitution d'un produit à un autre.

ARTICLE 9bis.

Lorsqu'une marque inscrite dans le Registre international sera transmise à une personne établie dans un pays contractant autre que le pays d'origine de la marque, la transmission sera notifiée au Bureau international par l'Administration de ce même pays d'origine. Le Bureau international, après avoir reçu l'assentiment de l'Administration à laquelle ressortit le nouveau titulaire, enregistrera la transmission, la notifiera aux autres Administrations et la publiera dans son journal en mentionnant, si possible, la date et le numéro d'enregistrement de la marque dans son nouveau pays d'origine.

Nulle transmission de marque inscrite dans le Registre international, faite au profit d'une personne non admise à déposer une marque internationale, ne sera enregistrée.

ARTICLE 9ter.

Les dispositions des articles 9 et 9bis concernant les transmissions n'ont point pour effet de modifier législations des pays contractants qui prohibent la transmission de la marque sans la cession simultanée de l'establissement industriel ou commercial dont elle distingue les produits.

ARTICLE 10.

Les Administrations régleront d'un commun accord les détails relatifs à l'exécution du présent Arrangement.

ARTICLE 11.

Les pays de l'Union pour la protection de la propriété industrielle qui n'ont pas pris part au présent Arrangement seront admis à y adhérer sur leur demande, et dans la forme prescrite par la Convention générale.

Dès que le Bureau international sera informé qu'un pays ou une de ses colonies a adhéré au présent Arrangement, il adressera à l'Administration de ce pays, conformément à l'article 3, une notification collective des marques qui, à ce moment, jouiront de la protection internationale.

Cette notification assurera, par elle-même, auxdites marques le bénéfice des précédentes dispositions sur le territoire du pays adhérent, et fera courir le délai d'un an pendant lequel l'Administration intéressée peut faire la déclaration prévue par l'article 5.

Toutefois, chaque pays en adhérant au présent Arrangement pourra déclarer que, sauf en ce qui concerne les marques internationales ayant déjà fait antérieurement dans ce pays l'objet d'un enregistrement national identique encore en vigueur et qui seront immédiatement reconnues sur la demande des intéressés, l'application de cet Acte sera limitée aux marques qui seront enregistrées à partir du jour où cette adhésion deviendra effective.

Cette déclaration dispensera le Bureau international de faire la notification collective susindiquée. Il se bornera à notifier les marques en faveur desquelles la demande d'être mis au bénéfice de l'exception prévue à l'alinéa précédent lui parviendra, avec les précisions nécessaires, dans le délai d'une année à partir de l'accession du nouveau pays.

Article 12.

Le présent Arrangement sera ratifié et les ratifications en seront déposées à La Haye, au plus tard le 1er mai 1928.

Il entrera en vigueur un mois après cette date et aura la même force et durée que la Convention générale.

Cet Acte remplacera, dans les rapports entre les pays qui l'auront ratifié, l'Arrangement de Madrid de 1891, revisé à Washington le 2 juin 1911. Toutefois, celui-ci restera en vigueur dans les rapports avec les pays qui n'auront pas ratifié le présent Acte.

EN FOI DE QUOI, les Plénipotentiaires respectifs ont signé le présent Arrangement.

Fait à *La Haye*, en un seul exemplaire, le *6 novembre 1925*.

The member countries of the restricted Union constituted by this Arrangement are:

Austria, Belgium, Brazil, Cuba, Czechoslovakia, Danzig, France (including Algeria and the Colonies), Germany, Hungary, Italy, Luxemburg, Morocco (French Zone), Mexico, the Netherlands (including the Dutch Indies, Surinam, and Curaçao), Portugal (including the Azores and Madeira), Rumania, Serb-Croat-Slovene State, Spain, Switzerland, Tunis, and Turkey.

Bei Fragen zur Produktsicherheit wenden Sie sich bitte an:
If you have any questions regarding product safety,
please contact:

Walter de Gruyter GmbH
Genthiner Straße 13
10785 Berlin
productsafety@degruyterbrill.com